Mathematics and the Study of Social Relations

BASIC IDEAS IN THE HUMAN SCIENCES
Editors: Alasdair MacIntyre and Patrick Doreian

BLACKBURN'S ISLE

BLACKBURN'S ISLE

by

DEREK NEVILLE

TERENCE DALTON LIMITED
LAVENHAM . SUFFOLK
1975

Published by
TERENCE DALTON LIMITED
LAVENHAM   SUFFOLK

ISBN 0 900963 40 9

370454

L BLA

Main Text Photoset in 11pt Baskerville Typeface

Printed in Great Britain at
THE LAVENHAM PRESS LIMITED
LAVENHAM   SUFFOLK

Contents

Index of Illustrations

To my wife Mary Neville
whose presence has been like a safe
anchorage in the ocean of experience.

Acknowledgements

I acknowledge with thanks the help given by the following:
The Mitchell Library of Sydney, N.S.W.
The Chairman and Members of the Lord Howe Island Board.
The British Museum.
Derek Weber, Editor of the *Geographical Magazine*.
W. R. Cornish of The London School of Economics and Political
   Science.
Tom Grix and Mrs Grix.
Mrs Brière of Colby.
Alexander Knapp.
The Norwich Central Reference Library.
Miss H. M. Bacon of the Norfolk and Norwich Subscription
   Library.
John Ferguson of Angus and Robertson.
Jean Brearley of Lord Howe Island.
Miss Anne Robertson, Liaison Librarian of the Mitchell Library in
   London.

Derek Neville,
Itteringham Mill,
Norfolk. 1975.

A brief history of Australia prior to 1788

According to Shaw, Australia is the oldest continent in the world, geologically speaking. "In the North West" he says, " a shield of land that has probably been above water for 1600 million years".

For centuries various explorers knew vaguely that there was a 'Great Southland'.

1420   Admiral Cheng Ho left China for Ceylon. A storm drove some vessels to to the South. Many years after Cheng Ho's return to China, a porcelain map was preserved at the National Museum at Peking. It showed a clear outline of the continent. There is little doubt that some of his ships had sailed round Australia.

1531   On a world map by Orontius Finaeus a great mass of land called *Terra Incognita* was for the first time given the name *Terra Australis*.

1540   The Portuguese claimed discovery of Australia.

1605   Captain Willem Jansz in a Dutch ship, *The Duyfhen* (Little Dove) sailed two hundred miles along the North Coast of Australia without knowing quite what he was doing. His crew landed and were the first white men to set foot on the Australian mainland.

1616   A Dutch ship *den Eendracht* of Amsterdam (Captain Dick Hartog) reached Western Australia. He left behind a metal plate on a post.

1618   Zeachern in the *Mauritius* discovered land in the North.

1619   Frederick Houtman discovered Abrolhos Island, West Australia.

1622   The Leeuwin, south-west cape of Australia, named after the ship *Leeuwin*.

1642   Tasman sailed round Australia, but he was too far south to find out much about it. He established that there was no land link between Australia and the Antarctic. (But see also 1420).

1688   William Dampier, an English pirate, landed from his ship *Cygnet* on the N.W. Coast and spent three months ashore.

1770   Captain Cook, in the *Endeavour*, made the first detailed and methodical discoveries. He charted the most important coastland in Australia, taking possession of it under the name of New South Wales. He and Joseph Banks dug a small well (which is still preserved) at a place they called Botany Bay.

1788   Captain Arthur Phillip arrived in Botany Bay in the *Supply*. The First Fleet follows into Sydney Cove.

Introduction

" Lieut. Ball then named the different parts of the Island. It is about 6 miles long and about 2 wide. At its south east end are two very high mountains which he named Mount Gower and Mount Lidgbird, the valley between them Erskine Valley. There is one on its South West side. The two small ones he called Callam Bay, the name of our surgeon, the other Hunter Bay after Captain John Hunter of the Sirius, the large bay Prince William Henry Bay and a small green island nearly in the middle of it Blackburn Isle.   "

— David Blackburn, in a letter written to his sister at St Michael's Coslany, Norwich, from H.M. Ship *Supply* at Sidney Cove, Port Jackson, Western Australia, 12th July, 1788.

CHAPTER ONE

A Casual Conversation

IT IS strange how a casual conversation can sometimes lead to extraordinary events. Words, whether written or spoken, engender a power that defies description.

Perhaps the most startling example of this kind of thing happened to me some time ago when a lady named Mrs Brière, visiting our home casually, spoke of some letters she had been reading. They were old letters, difficult to decipher. They had been written from Australia during the eighteenth century.

Among other things in a fairly varied life, I have long been in business as a secondhand book dealer. There are two kinds of people engaged in this sort of activity. There are dealers who regard books as a mere commodity, to be bought and sold like butter or beans. They export fine bindings by the yard, bestowing upon the purchaser something that will decorate his rooms without spoiling the effect of either carpets or curtains, at the same time giving him an intellectual status that we must suppose will satisfy his friends. There are others who love books for themselves; who are able to perceive the effort that went into their makings; who often stroke covers with gentle hands, turn pages with something approaching reverence, and exude a genuine joy over their discoveries. I like to think that I belong to this latter group.

You can therefore imagine my reaction upon hearing about these letters. A bookseller who knows his job always regards the year 1850 with guarded excitement. Take him back as far as 1820 and he stands at the entrance to the promised land. These letters were written before 1800. I had to see them.

They were written by a man named David Blackburn.

In due course I was shown a stiff binder containing some thirty or more letters. I looked at them for some ten minutes, warming even then to the faded writing and the parchment browning at its edges. It was not the moment to read them, but I dipped into several here and there and eventually asked if it might be possible to meet the owners of them. During the next day or so a few telephone calls were made and one morning I found myself sitting in the home of Mrs Grix at Burgh-next-Aylsham in the County of Norfolk. It was a quiet room with an open fire. Just the ticking of a clock—marking the endless passage of time.

The walls of this room were covered with horse-brasses—a magnificent collection belonging to Tom Grix, her eldest son. There were some four hundred of them, gathered mainly from private people over the last forty years, relics of a past when horses were the backbone of the country. It was certainly one of the finest horse-brass collections in the county—and probably the largest.

For Tom Attlee Grix was interested in things of the past. He had reason to be. His mother's side of the family could be traced back to Richard Coeur de Lion and it was because of this that he had his second name.

The story goes that a messenger one day arrived post-haste to see King Richard, to inform him that a child had been born to him by one of his mistresses, upon which the Monarch with a singular lack of tact enquired, "Where?"

"At Leigh, Sire!" replied the messenger.

So the child was called Attlee and since that time there has always been a child in the family bearing that name.

Upon the wall above the fireplace there were a number of framed silhouettes. They too, were old. One of them was of Elizabeth Blackburn (née Martineau). She was born on the 10th June, 1725. She died on the 8th November, 1805 at the age of eighty and was interred in the French Church at Norwich. She was David Blackburn's mother.

Another was of the Reverend John Blackburn of Newbury. He died on the 18th January, 1762 at the age of forty-one. He was David Blackburn's father. A third was of Elizabeth Burrows, wife of William Burrows (alderman of Norwich). She was born on the 30th April, 1760. She died 31st October, 1816 at the age of fifty-six. She was buried at Stoke Holy Cross in Norfolk. She was David Blackburn's sister. And a fourth was of David Blackburn himself, a quiet unassuming man whose letters home are now a part of history.

Mrs Grix herself, lively and intelligent at the age of eighty-five, made me a cup of tea while I sat there among the memories that were without beginning or end. At one point, the front door opened and a voice said: "Post." I got the letters for her and she sat opening them while I thought of those other letters written long ago, from a far-off land.

Far away, those days! But this room, filled as it was with memories, linked 1972 with 1792 in more ways than one.

How was it that these letters came to be here at all? I am never very good at family relationships. They muddle me. Once I get beyond a straight grandparent, I get confused. But by dint of painstaking perseverance, I have at last straightened out these circumstances. Put in simple terms, they are as follows:

The Reverend John Blackburn of Newbury married Elizabeth Martineau and they had at least three children, David Blackburn, Margaret Blackburn and Elizabeth Blackburn.

Elizabeth Blackburn married William Burrows, an Alderman of Norwich, and these were the great grandparents of Mrs Grix.

Mrs Grix's grandmother lived at The Dower House in the village of Heydon, Norfolk. She died there and her tombstone is to be found in the churchyard.

Her daughter married a Mr Ready in 1884. (His brother, Oliver Ready, wrote *Life and Sport on the Norfolk Broads,* published by T. Werner Laurie and also *Life and Sport in China;* — Chapman & Hall, 1903.) They moved to Aldeby in Suffolk where Mrs Grix was born. After that the family moved to Bridgham, near Thetford, Norfolk, where her father was rather an unsuccessful farmer. He left farming eventually and moved to The Mill House at Burgh. At that time the Mill itself was a separate entity. Mary Ready, of course, paid occasional visits to the Mill so near to her home — to buy corn or flour, and it was out of these visits that romance sprung. Eventually she married James Grix who was, at that time, employed there. They lived in the Mill House and eventually acquired both properties.

Burgh Mill is now one of the few working mills left in Norfolk and the business is run by Michael Grix who lives in a pleasant house beside it. It is used for the manufacture of cattle food, the machinery being driven partly by water and partly by diesel engine.

You can stand there, as I have done, with the sun shining down on the water of the Bure, and see the great wheel dripping as it turns — surely one of the loveliest sights left in a world that is gradually being governed by computers.

So it was here — to this Mill House by the Bure — to this quiet industrious family that these letters came down through the years, by right of inheritance. A family where old things are loved for themselves and in whose hands they have been preserved as treasures.

And in a corner of this very room — as a vivid reminder of those harsh days when David Blackburn went with the First Fleet, stood a curious instrument — a long stout handle, stained, weather-beaten and worn smooth with use, and, at one end, the knotted ropes with all their dreadful implications. It was a cat-o'-nine tails. Without much doubt it was used on board H.M. Armed Tender *Supply*.

All lives are islands, related to the mainland of humanity by the ocean of time. But in this case, the link was more definite than usual. Out of the past there had emerged these letters, tangible things, the handwriting now faded and difficult to read, but each one written by a long gone hand, put into its envelope and despatched by coach and by sailing vessel across half the world.

It seemed to me that they should be preserved, if possible. For, heaven knows, the past and its more leisurely ways is in ever-increasing danger of being submerged by the crescendo of modern living. There is less and less time to think quietly as innumerable pressures are brought to bear upon us.

Recently, a friend of ours named Cecil Meadows, who is something of an authority on oil lamps, gave us a talk at our home. About thirty people came and we all listened to him as he described the impressive assembly of old lamps on display. I found myself thinking, during that evening, of those old times. Perhaps they were hard. No doubt they were. Perhaps we have progressed. No doubt we have. But there were certain compensations, as I suppose there always are. And perhaps the greatest lay in the fact that leisure, in those days, was leisure, as distinct from being a two minute break for a commercial. With the curtains drawn, and the lamps lit, and the fire blazing, there must have been more time for reflection.

Certainly, these letters had to be preserved and it was eventually agreed that I should write a book around them, providing, as it were, a suitable literary frame for them. When I left the house at Burgh, I was entrusted with the binder — having promised to take the utmost care of it and never to let it out of my hands.

So I went home, put the letters safely away in a dark cupboard and left them there for six weeks.

There came a morning when I took them out again and began the task of getting them sorted out.

Eventually I had a typewritten file of the letters — all in date order, all in duplicate. I regarded them somewhat glumly. I did not know, at that moment, that they were to prove the entry to a new world.

From that day onwards, for the next twelve months I lived with these letters. They soaked into my being and carried me back across nearly two hundred years. They were to become an obsession with me, a driving force that would give me no rest until the task was done.

CHAPTER TWO

The Early Years

THE beginnings of David Blackburn are shrouded in obscurity and we know very little about him as far as his early years are concerned. He was born in Newbury, Berkshire, on the 1st January, 1753. As we have seen, he was the eldest son of the Reverend John Blackburn of Newbury and of his wife Elizabeth née Martineau, a Norwich woman.

He spent his first nine years in Newbury. At that point, his father died and his widowed mother moved back to the City of Norwich where, no doubt, she had many friends.

As he grew from boyhood to manhood, he would have seen various historic events taking place in the City in which he lived. He would have seen the names of the streets and highways fixed up for the first time. He would probably have remembered a violent storm in 1770 when the windmills of Happisburgh, Postwick and Strogshall were all blown down. The Assembly House would have been new, for it was built on the site of Chapelfield House in 1754, when he was a year old. Twelve months later, the first Bank was opened in the City.

When he first arrived in Norwich, the *Norfolk Chronicle* was in its first year of publication. He was ten years old when the first hackney coach was set up in Norwich by one, William Huggins. In fact, the first mail coach running between Norwich and London was not established until 1785. This coach succeeded in completing the distance of 108 miles in fifteen hours and no doubt letters sent from Norwich reached their destinations more rapidly than they do nowadays!

Blackburn was seven years old when George II died on the 25th October, 1760. George III was proclaimed King in Norwich on the 29th October by the Mayor and Corporation, according to A. T. Baine in his history of Norwich. Though, curiously enough, Browne, in a similar history, says the 30th October. Perhaps the celebrations extended into the small hours! However, both histories agree that the Coronation was celebrated with great splendour in Norfolk on the 22nd September, 1761.

He was eighteen years old when the foundation of the Norfolk and Norwich Hospital was laid by William Fellowes, and thirty-one years of age before the first Public Library was opened in Norwich in the old Library room, formerly over the entrance to St Andrews Hall.

Blackburn would probably have known about William Crotch* who, in 1778 astounded a large company at Norwich with a precocity almost unparalleled in music, by performing on the organ at about three years of age.

No doubt he would have heard the peal of 5,170 changes rung on the twelve bells of St Martin's, Mancroft, in four hours and one minute — the first attempt of its kind. However, when Mrs Siddons performed on eight nights at the Theatre Royal in 1787, he was not there. He had left Norwich to begin his adventures which are the subject of this book.

*   *   *

Before we go with him, it is desirable that we take a more general look at Norwich — and indeed England — during the last quarter of the eighteenth century. The important thing is to understand the general conditions that prevailed as he grew up.

The world into which David Blackburn was born was a very different world from the one we know. The England of that time was a dreadful place for any who were poor and hungry. The theft of five shillings was punishable by death and eighteen out of every twenty who were hanged in London were under the age of twenty-one.

How very poor the people were may be judged by the following extract from the history of Norwich by P. Browne: —

"1766, 27th September, about noon broke out among the lower class of inhabitants, a dreadful riot, occasioned by a scarcity of provisions. The riotors damaged the houses and destroyed the

---

William Crotch by Jonathan Rennert, published by Terence Dalton Limited, Lavenham, 1975.

furniture of several bakers, pulled down part of the new mills, and destroyed a large quantity of flour there. They likewise burned to the ground a large malthouse without Conisford-gate. They were suppressed the next day, about five in the afternoon, whilst they were destroying a baker's house in Tombland, by the magistrates and inhabitants, without the assistance of the military. Thirty of the ringleaders were taken and tried for the offence at an Assize holden by special commission on the first day of December following. Eight received sentence of death, but only two were ordered for execution."

These two were executed on the following 10th January.

The lot of poor people was quite unbelievable — not only at that particular time, but even into the first half of the nineteenth century.

In the introduction to *Margaret Catchpole* by Richard Cobbold, Clement Shorter commended the book for giving us a glimpse of the cruel criminal law of the eighteenth century. He went on:

"Hanging for small offences went on for years after this, until, indeed, public opinion was revolted by the case of a young married woman who in Ludgate Hill lifted a piece of cloth from the counter. She hesitated and then put it down again. But she had been seen, and was arrested, tried, condemned, and hanged, although it was clearly proved that her husband had been seized by a press-gang and that her babe cried for bread".

There is also an interesting footnote to this introduction as follows:

"The punishment of death for horse-stealing was abolished in 1832, but in 1833 a little boy of nine who pushed a stick through a cracked window and pulled out some painters' colours worth twopence was sentenced to death".

Probably neither of these died altogether in vain. The public conscience began to make itself felt after such horrors and since 1838 no person has been hanged in England for any offence other than murder or treason.

Norwich was very far from the splendid City that it is today. The population would have been about 40,000 and many of the people were poor beyond belief. Had it not been, in fact, for the large numbers of starving people in England at that time, most of them hopelessly overwhelmed by their circumstances, there would have been no fleet sailing to the great unknown land in the South.

Smuggling was abundant, even in broad daylight. During the first half of the eighteenth century, according to William Durrant Cooper, who was an authority on the subject:

"...the daring of the smugglers grew with the impunity with which they were enabled to act. Large gangs of twenty, forty, fifty, even one hundred, rode, with guns, bludgeons and clubs, throughout the country, setting every one at defiance, and awing all the quiet inhabitants..."

Again:

"In 1779, it became necessary to pass another act against smuggling; and, in a pamphlet making the new law known,* it is stated that the practice of smuggling had made such rapid strides from the sea-coasts into the very heart of the country, pervading every city, town and village, as to have brought universal distress on the fair dealer; that the greater part of the 3,867,500 gallons distilled annually at Schiedam, was to be smuggled into England; that a distillery had lately been set up for making Geneva, for the same purpose, at Dunkirk; that the French imported five or six millions of pounds of tea, the greatest part of which was to be smuggled here; that the trade of Dunkirk was mostly carried on by smugglers, in vessels not only large, but so well constructed for sailing, that seldom one of them was captured; that in many places near the sea, the farmer was unable to find hands to do his work, whilst great numbers were employed in smuggling goods from one part of the country to another; and that the smugglers paid for what they bought in cash, or by the illicit exportation of English wool, no other articles of any consequence being carried aboard by them."*

In these days of semi-enlightenment, it is fairly easy to see that many crimes spring from broken homes and from unfortunate environments. In those days, almost all environment, except among the very rich, was unfortunate. Moreover, the laws of England were

---

*Advice to the Unwary, 1780.
*Vol. X. Sussex Archaeological Collection.

very easily broken at that time. An offence against property—no matter the cause—merited the most vicious retaliations by authority and most offenders were themselves the victims of circumstance, poor beyond belief, homeless and overwhelmed.

This was the background of the early years of David Blackburn. These were the facts which, more than any other, were to decide his destiny.

CHAPTER THREE

The Great Southland

THE land we now know as Australia was first seen by Captain Cook on the morning of the 19th April, 1770. It would be quite wrong to say that he discovered it, for the existence of a vast land to the South had been rumoured since the eighth century.

In 1531, on a world map by Orontius Finaeus, a great land mass which had been called Terra Incognita is for the first time given the name *Terra Australis*. This fact means nothing, however, in regard to the actual discovery of Australia. The word *Australia* simply means "southern". The great southland was the name given to a vague mass of land which was thought to exist south of Capricorn.

Mendana (1568) voyaged with the precise intention of trying to discover the great continent. He discovered the Solomon Islands and an attempt was, in fact, made to colonise them.

A Dutch ship, the *Duyfhen,* (1605) achieved fame by sailing some 200 miles along the north coast of Australia without knowing precisely what they were doing. And in the museum in Amsterdam is a pewter utensil on which an inscription in Dutch says: "A.D. 1616 on the 25th October, there arrived here the ship 'den Eendraght' of Amsterdam; skipper Dirk Hartog."

This was discovered in Western Australia in 1697.

The first man to circumnavigate Australia was the Dutchman, Tasman, 1642. He discovered both Tasmania and New Zealand but he was too far south of the great land mass of Australia to solve anything other than that there was no land link between the Australian land and the Antarctic.

After Tasman there were no more important explorations in Australian waters for over a hundred years and it was left to Captain Cook, 1769-1770, to chart the most important coastland in Australia. It was during this voyage that he found a satisfactory harbour of which both he and Joseph Banks spoke highly, and they named it Botany Bay. They dug a small well there which is still preserved.

This was the place, and this was the hour in which Australia, as we know it today, can be said to have had its real beginning. For it was the high commendation of Captain Cook and his colleagues which was to result in the founding of the first settlement some eighteen years later. It was this place—Botany Bay—in which Australia had its real beginning.

According to Shaw, Australia is the oldest continent in the world, geologically speaking. "In the North-West," he writes, "is a shield of land that has probably been above water for 1,600 million years."

Curiously enough, it was never inhabited by any but Stone Age people until the time with which this book is concerned, and even then it is improbable that anything would have been done but for a special need that arose in England.

How strange are the events that shape history! The area of England is about 50,000 square miles. Australia has something approaching 3,000,000 square miles. All the counties of England could be laid upon its surface sixty times. Even New South Wales itself is six times larger than England. Yet the basic driving force behind the development of the whole of Australia lay in the domestic troubles of the British Government.

The outcome of the American War of Independence had had far-reaching effects upon Britain. There were, of course, a large number of Americans who had sided with Britain and who felt themselves to be no longer exactly welcome on the American mainland. A suggestion put forward in 1783 was that a Colony should be established for them in Australia and for a time serious consideration was given to this project. But there were interminable delays and the Colonists were in no mood for them. Most probably, they could not afford such delays even if they had wanted to wait. So they moved elsewhere—mainly to Canada—some to Holland.

One cannot help but wonder whether the course of history might have been changed had this original plan gone forward. Certainly it is safe to say that the ties between the U.S.A. and Australia would have been greatly strengthened and that the advancement of the Continent would have been accelerated in terms of both trade and growth when the immediate animosities had died down. But it was not to be; and soon the British authorities began to think in new terms.

The outcome of the American War of Independence had had another profound effect quite apart from the banished colonists.

For some time it had been the practice of Great Britain to send convicts to one or other of the American Colonies. This was no longer possible and meanwhile, as we have seen, the English prisons became hopelessly overcrowded.

It was therefore put forward in certain quarters that the territory discovered by Captain Cook in 1770 should be used for the purpose of accommodating criminals who were proving an embarrassment in England.

It is, I believe, no mere coincidence that this idea should have been put forward at a time when numbers of people were beginning to be horrified at the callousness with which those who broke the law — even in minor ways — were treated. Quite apart from the obvious need of a safe place to put them — both out of sight and of mind — the very idea of transportation had about it a tinge of mercy and in the years that followed there were to be many unctuous utterances designed to reveal mere convenience disguised as compassion.

Professor Spate of the Australian National University in his splendidly well-written book *Australia* — surely a literary work in itself — is inclined to think that *settlement* itself was probably much more a motive than it is usually held to be. To some degree he is probably right. Certainly the British were not, as a rule, apt to ignore commercial opportunities. But there is reason to believe that it was more than helpful to the judiciary in England to have a place as far as possible to which they could send those who embarrassed them — and at the same time assume, in the very act of doing so, the mantle of compassion.

In 1786, Arthur Phillip was chosen by Lord Sydney, Secretary of State for the Home Department, as Captain-General of an expedition to New South Wales and Governor of the settlement it was intended to establish there.

Nobody quite knows exactly why he was chosen. He had certainly had some experience in the Navy — but in 1763 he had retired with the rank of Lieutenant on half pay to farm land near Lyndhurst, Hampshire, in Southern England. It is thought that his knowledge of farming may even have been a factor contributing to his appointment.

Certainly, he was the man for the job. He was a good organiser and a person of both integrity and imagination. Under his leadership as the first Governor of New South Wales he was able to bring new meaning to bear upon an exercise that had been initiated primarily for the purpose of finding a dumping-ground for convicted persons or troublesome subjects.

Although fifty-four years were to pass before the transport scheme was finally abandoned, Governor Phillip was able, at least, to conduct affairs in such a way that the initial difficulties, which were tremendous, were surmounted.

(i)   Captain James Cook who landed at Botany Bay on 29th April, 1770.

Australian Information Service Photograph

(ii)   Captain Cook proclaiming New South Wales a British possession, Botany Bay, 1770.

Australian Information Service

(iii) The *Endeavour* of Captain Cook — a model in Whitby Museum. Built at Whitby as the *Earl of Pembroke* in 1764 as a collier bark.

Roger Finch

(iv) Abel Tasman, after a portrait by van der Helst.

(v) Cottage built at Great Ayton, Yorkshire by parents of Captain Cook in 1755. Removed to present site in Fitzroy Gardens, Melbourne as gift of Mr Russell Grimwade of Melbourne in 1934.

Australian Information Service

(vi) Porstmouth drawn by J. M. W. Turner, R.A. and engraved by Thomas Lupton.

(vii) The *Supply* and other ships, including H.M.S. *Sirius* after arrival at Botany Bay from a drawing by R. Cleveley engraved by T. Medland.

National Maritime Museum, Greenwich

(viii)   Foundation of Sydney by Captain Arthur Phillip. Inspecting the convict settlers.
By R. Caton Woodville, 1903.
Mansell Collection

(ix)   Captain Arthur Phillip, first Governor of the New South Wales and commander of the
        fleet which reached Botany Bay on 18th January 1788. He unfurled the British flag on
        shores of Port Jackson on 26th January, now celebrated as Australia Day.

                                                Australian News and Information Bureau

CHAPTER FOUR

Prelude to Departure

THIS, then, was the situation in 1787. For the first time the eyes of the British Government were turned towards Botany Bay as a far distant carpet under which might be swept the overflow from the jails and the prison hulks. At the same time, there could be steps taken to found a Settlement there—and perhaps a trading station on Norfolk Island which had already received a favourable report from Captain Cook.

And it is in the midst of this situation that we first come across David Blackburn. He is a man now. He is thirty-four years of age. He has joined the Navy and he is waiting for a ship. Early in the year 1787 he writes a letter from the *Black Bull,* Bishopsgate to his sister Margaret to whom he is deeply attached. He is obviously very short of money and in need of a commission. He stands 226th on the Navy list—high enough to be called to service—but not high enough to be given half pay without a post. So he is taking active steps to find one.

Twenty-three days later he writes to his mother from London with the first real news. It is the 4th April, 1787. On that day he had been sent for by the Navy Office where he was given a warrant appointing him Master of H.M. Armed Tender *Supply*—bound for Botany Bay!

Two things are very apparent in this letter. The first is haste. He is due to sail in a few days and, at this moment, he has not even got his sea-chest. In fact, he is unprepared in many ways, having no linen, books, charts—and, above all, money. He is very anxious to acquire ten pounds and he wonders whether his mother could supply it.

The second thing that becomes clear in this letter is Blackburn's attitude to the whole project. He is a reluctant mariner, if ever there was one.

This fact is borne out by his next letter, written two days later to his sister, again from London. In this, he explains that he has tried in vain to get his warrant changed, but with no success. Indeed, he has been told in no uncertain terms that if he refuses to go he will be struck off the Navy List and will almost certainly get no further employment until every other Master has been provided for.

It is clear that the Navy Board is well aware of its power. They offer him the miserable sum of five pounds per month—instead of the seven pounds monthly to which he is justly entitled. Take it—or leave it!

However, there is *some* good news! His Aunt Martineau has produced the ten pounds and with it he has purchased a dozen new shirts, a coat, six pairs of shoes, a dozen pairs of stockings and also various charts! Inflation, in those days, was merely the way to insert hot air into a balloon! One of those charts would, today, be worth a hundred pounds!

In this letter, too, there is the first mention of his commander. He is to be Lieutenant H. L. Ball, an old ship mate of Blackburn's from the *Victory*.

Little did he know as he wrote the letter a few hours before leaving to join his ship at Portsmouth, that he and Ball would be making history as they sailed the *Supply* across unknown seas to an unknown land.

*　　*　　*

It is the 10th April, 1787. Blackburn has arrived at Portsmouth, where his address is given as c/o Mr Lads, The White Hart, Point Street.

Again he writes to his sister, a somewhat poignant letter, a letter which, in the light of after events, is filled with prescience. He is very anxious to see his sister once more before he sails. Could she possibly call to see him on her way to Newbury? He is even willing to spend a guinea and a half for "so desirable a satisfaction". And this from a man who, but a few days before had been penniless!

He is now resigned to the trip. "It is therefore my Duty to obey without murmuring" he writes, "and I shall make it my study to go through my Duty with cheerfulness."

He still does not know when they will sail. "It is supposed to be the middle or latter end of this month." However, his chest has arrived safely and "it goes on board tonight and tomorrow I go on board myself."

Five days later, on the 15th April, 1787, Blackburn again writes to his sister, this time from the *Supply*. It is apparent that she is not responding to his request for a last meeting before the ship sails. "You have said enough to convince me that it is not essentially necessary for you to come to Portsmouth and that seeing you again before I sail could not be to any advantage to either and the objections you mention, particularly your cold, has put it out of my power to wish you to take the journey." Nevertheless, his hope still lingers. "...when you and our Mother arrive in London, your cold better and she should express a wish to come to Portsmouth with you, I hope I shall then see you..."

But five days later his flickering hopes are dead. In a further letter to his sister he writes: "It will be impossible for me to get leave of absence any further from the ship than Portsmouth, even if you were now in London, and I relinquish my wish of seeing you here, for great as the pleasure would be in seeing you, there must come a parting painful to us both..."

He never saw his sister Margaret Blackburn again.

There were three more swift letters from him on the 2nd, 6th, and 9th May.

On the 6th he says "the whole fleet are ready for sea at a day's notice."

On the 9th he writes "Friday is the day fixed for our sailing if the wind will permit." This was the last letter he wrote to his sister from England.

Apparently, the wind did not permit. It was Saturday, 13th May 1787 when the Fleet sailed. Then, with the wind freshening, the sails of the *Supply* were set towards a far distant land at the very dawn of its history.

CHAPTER FIVE

The Journey There

THE TERM *master* can be confusing, if it is not properly understood. It was not, as might be supposed, the highest rank in the ship. It meant that Blackburn was a navigating officer immediately under the rank of Lieutenant. Nevertheless, it was a very important position to hold on such a ship as the *Supply* which, as events unfolded, was to find a very real place in the history of Australia.

The little armed tender of 170 tons was one of the only two Naval vessels accompanying the fleet which also contained six transports and three store ships, and it might be as well to note here the precise details of the two naval vessels.

The Flagship, bearing the Commodore, Captain Arthur Phillip, was H.M.S. *Sirius,* 540 tons. The rest of the crew were as follows: — Captain—Captain John Hunter; Surgeon—Charles Bouchier Wogan; 1st Lieutenant—William Bradley; 2nd Lieutenant—Philip Gidley King; 3rd Lieutenant—George William Maxwell; Master—James Keltie; Midshipmen—Neuton Fowell, Francis Hill, Henry Waterhouse, Henry Brewer; Master's Mate—James Cunningham; Mate—Daniel Southwell; Surgeon's Mate—Thomas Jamison; Purser—John Palmer.

H.M.S. *Supply:* — 170 tons. Commander—Lieutenant Henry Lidgbird Ball; Surgeon—James Callam; Master—David Blackburn; Carpenter—Robinson Reed; Boatswain—Peter Gould.

The remaining ships in the fleet were: *Alexander* 448 tons; *Friendship* 276 tons; *Scarborough* 420 tons; *Prince of Wales* 334 tons; *Charlotte* 339 tons; *Lady Penrhyn* 331 tons; *Borrowdale* 274 tons; *Golden Grove* 353 tons and *Fishburn* 378 tons.

* * *

We tend to grumble sometimes, at the efforts of our various governments although, I suppose, they are no less than we deserve.

Yet one doubts whether any government in modern times has

made such palpable errors as were made by the British Government of 1786/7.

At first sight, it might not seem to have been Sydney's fault. In a directive addressed to both the Treasury and the Admiralty, he wrote orders:

> "That you do forthwith take such measures as may be necessary for providing a proper number of vessels for the conveyance of seven hundred and fifty convicts* to Botany Bay, together with such provisions, necessaries, and implements for agriculture as may be necessary for their use after their arrival."

The fact remains, however, that preparations were badly organised. In spite of Cook's glowing recommendation of Botany Bay as the ideal spot for a settlement (a viewpoint which was to prove more than over-optimistic) nothing had been done for years. The American colonists had been neglected. Indeed, the whole idea of any positive settlement had been neglected. Suddenly, however, the need became urgent. The hulks and prisons were overflowing. The perpetual hangings were beginning to sicken small sections of the public conscience. For, perhaps, the first time those in authority gave a long hard look at the idea of making some use of the southland and the idea of conveying convicts to it was suddenly the obvious thing to do. The moment their lordships turned their gaze upon this easy way out of a vexatious and ever-increasing problem — it seemed clear beyond any doubt. Banishment for a long period — even for life — from their country of birth would be a real deterrent. (At a later period convicted persons frequently declared that they would rather die than be transported to an unknown land they feared); it would empty the jails; in the end it would be an economy, for the new land would be self-sufficient; it would seem merciful (no doubt in many instances, it would be a genuine act of mercy, for not

---

*The actual number of convicts conveyed by the first fleet has been much in dispute. Dr Eris O'Brien in *The Foundation of Australia* decided upon seven hundred and fifty-nine convicts comprising 568 men and 191 women with 13 of their children. It should be noted, however, that David Blackburn states specifically in his letter dated 2nd September — "with convicts viz. 596 men and 267 women." This adds up to 863 and shows a very great difference — an increase of 91. Blackburn's letter was written seven and a half months after sailing. One supposes that there would have been some births and that such additions were included. But 91 births from 191 women — many over child-bearing age is too much to expect. In fact, Blackburn in the same letter specifically states: "There have been 8 or 10 births."

all the judiciary were devoid of feeling); convict labour would be used for the establishment of the settlement; and, finally, the whole project might very well result in an ultimate expansion of trade, beyond the wildest dream of Sydney and his colleagues.

There were two other considerations, at least. One was the need to colonise before other nations got round to it. The other was the added attraction of forming a trading post on Norfolk Island. A proposal to this effect had, in fact, been made to the East India Company in 1785 — but nothing had come of it in spite of the fact that Captain Cook had given a very favourable report of it and that there were known to be pines growing there suitable for spars for the Royal Navy.

Once these facts had been duly absorbed, preparations were speeded up inordinately.

The wisdom of hindsight is easy — but when one thinks of the mistakes made and the risks that were taken in consequence the mind boggles. The fact that there were no actual overseers for the convicts may be forgiven; no doubt there were plenty of marines who could undertake such duties. But there was, in fact, another small oversight. Hardly any ammunition was provided for the marines' muskets!

The natives, as it transpired, were little trouble. Had this not been so the whole expedition might well have foundered during its first years in New South Wales.

Furthermore, no skilled tradesmen were included in the party. In a new harsh land where the utmost improvisation would undoubtedly be called for, no real attempt had been made to cover such contingencies as might demand the services of the specialist!

The following is quoted from *The New World of the South* by W. H. Fitchett (1913):

"Great Britain did not spare money in the equipment of the first fleet. There was expended on it nearly £190,000. A return dated 1793, when the settlement in Australia had been in existence five years, showed that its average cost to the mother-land was £78,840 per annum, and this rose to a vastly greater scale in later years. But though there was much cash spent on the equipment of the first fleet, there was a mournful lack of common sense displayed in the process. The manifest of the transports shows such items as 700 steel blades, 700 gimlets,

8,000 fish-hooks, etc., down to 'three dozen flat-iron candle-sticks,' 'three snuffers,' and '*one* Bible'! But the list of things *forgotten* is long and melancholy. The very cartridges for the muskets of the marines were forgotten; the clothes for the women-convicts — and there were nearly 200* of them — were left behind. No carpenters or bricklayers were sent out for the erection of houses, no agriculturists to grow wheat, and no superintendents for the purpose of keeping the convicts in order. Phillip, who was in command of the fleet, had to organise a staff of superintendents from amongst the convicts themselves.

No teacher or schoolmaster was included in the staff. Two Roman Catholic priests, who petitioned to be allowed to accompany the convicts — nearly half the number being of their religion — did not even receive a reply to their application. One minister of religion only was sent out, the Rev. Richard Johnson, 'one of the people called Methodists,' to use the phrase employed by Major Grose, who was in command of the marines.

The very records of the sentences of the convicts were forgotten. When the convicts were shipped they were transferred on terms of servitude, as a legal form, to the masters of the transports. Phillip was instructed, when the transports were discharged, to secure an assignment to himself of the servitude of each convict from the master of the transport. But all the official papers were left behind. Nobody could tell about any given convict, the nature of his offence, the date of his conviction, or the term for which he had been transported. Of the shovels and other tools on board the ships, Phillip records that they were 'the worst ever seen, as bad as ever were sent out for barter on the coast of Guinea. The seed was for the most part weevily and incapable of growth. Never was such a catalogue of omissions and disappointments.'"

However, on Sunday 13th May, 1787, the little fleet of eleven ships set sail from Portsmouth. Three weeks later they had reached Teneriffe and David Blackburn wrote to his sister in Norwich. His letter was dated 5th June, 1787.

It was not much of a letter, but this was understandable since they

---

*267 according to Blackburn.

were only stopping to take in water and wine and they were to sail within a few days for Rio de Janeiro on their way to the Cape.

In fact, they reached Rio on the 6th August and did not leave again until Tuesday 4th September — the long stay being accounted for by the fact that the rigging of some ships was refitted. It was during this stay that Blackburn wrote his first long letter home. He gave a short account of the voyage to this point, and also a useful description of Rio de Janeiro.

To quote the letters in full at this point would be something of an intrusion in the text and for this reason, the entire collection of the Blackburn letters has been made into an Appendix where they can all be found in date order at the end of the book.

One point, however, should be made from this particular letter, since it is relevant to our story. Regarding the convicts themselves, Blackburn wrote:

> "They are all very healthy, having in all from their first embarkation buried only 20 men and 2 women and there has been 8 or 10 births, chiefly females. I cannot quit this subject without saying that the health of the convicts may in a great measure be attributed to the humanity of the Governor, who gives them every indulgence their situation will admit of, none of them are confined in chains or even under the deck by day, except such whose behaviour deserves such punishment and they are constantly supplied with fresh provisions, fruit and vegetables."

The humane treatment of the convicts by Captain Phillip is significant. The twenty-two deaths out of a total of 750 odd is not great. Many of them would have been sick, or without much will to live before they started. The point worth noting is that Phillip had the welfare of his cargo in hand. Not everybody in authority in those days cared very much.

For instance, it may not be generally known that the writer of the well-known hymn "How sweet the name of Jesus sounds" was himself a slave-dealer and the fact remains that John Newton, in my humble opinion, was capable of more self-deception than I have ever come across in my contact with religious people. The hymns he wrote are very well known, of course. This particular hymn goes on to say:

> "It makes the wounded spirit whole
> And calms the troubled breast;

'Tis manna to the hungry soul,
And to the weary rest."

Nevertheless, the fact remains that John Newton was engaged not only in the Slave Trade but in the Guinea Slave Trade. This was the very worst part of the slave business for it meant that the private adventurers were admitted freely to the trade by the Government. The Royal African Company's affairs declined and the whole aspect of the Slave Trade, bad as it was, changed for the worse.

It was during this period of the Slave Trade that John Newton was operating. In commenting on and quoting from Newton's Memoirs F. A. J. Utting in *The Story of Sierra Leone* says;

"The slaves were not always docile and he tells how on the voyage, 'The slaves on board were likewise frequently plotting insurrections, and were sometimes upon the very brink of mischief; but it was always disclosed in due time.'

'The most remarkable passage in his memoirs is the following: — 'I never knew sweeter or more frequent hours of divine communion, than in my last two voyages to Guinea...'

"Remember that beneath his cabin were the crowded wretches he had captured to sell as slaves!"

How we deceive ourselves when the profit motive takes over!

It would have been very easy for Phillip, in his position of power, to have proved hard or even brutal in his treatment of the prisoners. He had been given almost unlimited power, both civil and military, but he used it well. The following note from an Australian Encyclopaedia says much in a few words:

"Phillip was a slight dark-complexioned man of less than average height, quick in manner, self-controlled and courageous. His task was to make a settlement in a wilderness with few and imperfect tools, and a host of broken men to use them. He had, however, the determination that enables a man to make the best of bad conditions. His strong sense of duty and the fact that he had no gift of getting on with people made him unpopular, and he received little help from some of his subordinates. But, steadfast in mind, idealistic and modest, he had imagination enough to conceive what the settlement might become, and the common sense to realise what at the moment was possible and expedient. When almost everyone was complaining, he never himself complained; when all feared disaster he could still go on with his work. He was sent out to found a convict settlement and he laid the foundations of a nation."

*   *   *

From Rio, the fleet sailed on across the Pacific Ocean to the Cape of Good Hope where they arrived on Sunday 14th October, after a pleasant voyage without incident.

They stayed at the Cape a month during which time they took on water and a large quantity of livestock for the Colony.

"Could you see the Supply" wrote Blackburn to his sister, "she would put you in mind of Noah's Ark, except that we have no woman on board."

This letter, dated 9th November, 1787, was the last to be written on the actual journey to Botany Bay. Five days later, the fleet sailed on the last tremendous stage of nearly 9,000 miles. There would be no place of refuge now, no haven of any sort. They were sailing virtually unknown seas and they were going to an unknown land. The next letter was to be written more than eight months later from Sidney Cove. During this time much had happened and a great deal of history had been made by a small body of determined men.

CHAPTER SIX

The *Supply* Sails to Norfolk Island

THE facts concerning the first few weeks of the First Settlement have been recorded in so many books that very little need be said about them here.

The little *Supply* was the first ship to arrive at Botany Bay on the 18th January, 1788, the Governor having left his Flagship to board her as she was faster than the other vessels. In fact, the rest of the Fleet did not arrive until the 20th.

So David Blackburn was among those who first stepped ashore at the founding of Australia. And three days later the Governor, Captain Hunter, James Keltie and David Blackburn went along the coast to the northward to find Sydney Bay and to name Port Jackson. There they settled the whole colony. There they built the first houses and the first stockades. It was there, around one of the great natural harbours of the world, that Australia was born.

It was David Blackburn who navigated the whole fleet up that harbour to a point six miles from its entrance — Sydney Cove.

Less than a month later — on the 14th February, 1788 to be precise — the *Supply* at the orders of Governor Phillip, set out on another historic voyage — for the purpose of settling a colony on Norfolk Island. At the beginning of February, they began taking on board six months provisions and all necessary implements that could be spared and they also took with them a surgeon, a midshipman, a master weaver, nine male convicts and six women convicts.

Governor Phillip had, in his initial directive, been ordered by the British Government, to form a colony on Norfolk Island and he now acted with commendable speed. To have sent out this further expedition from Port Jackson less than a month after arrival, needed both courage and foresight. He could ill spare the ship and the men who were upon it and he must have known that there was always the risk that the *Supply* would never return. But it had to be done, and Phillip saw that it ought to be done swiftly.

Norfolk Island, with an area of about 13 square miles, lies 930 miles to the north-east of Sydney. It was to be a lifeline — but a distant lifeline indeed. One thing about the island was already known and had been reported by Cook some years before. There were tall firs growing there. The importance of this to sailors in those distant waters was tremendous. For these firs would provide the timbers they needed — especially for masts.

So it was to Norfolk Island that David Blackburn went next under the command of Lieutenant Henry Lidgbird Ball. They carried with them the following:

> Lieutenant King who had been made Superintendent and
> Commandant of Norfolk Island.
> Mr Jamison, Surgeon — First Mate of the *Sirius*.
> T. Turnpenny Altree — Assistant to the Surgeon.
> James Cunningham — Master's Mate of the *Sirius*.
> Roger Morley — a master weaver.
> William Westbrook — a sawyer.
> Two mariners named Kerridge and Batchelor.

There were six women convicts: Elizabeth Lee, Elizabeth Hipsley, Elizabeth Colley, Olivia Gascoin, Ann Innett and Susan Gough.

Also nine male convicts: Charles McClellan, Richard Widdicombe, Edward Garth, Edward Westlake, John Mortimer, Noah Mortimer, Nathaniel Lucas and two others unknown.

All the convicts who went to Norfolk Island for the purpose of settlement there were carefully chosen by Lieutenant King in consultation with Surgeon Bowes. They were chosen because of their good behaviour during the voyage from England. They were now offered many improvements upon their former situation. King told them that if they misbehaved he himself would not punish them — but would simply send them back to Port Jackson — which would be a punishment in itself — where they would be dealt with. But if they co-operated, it would be very much to their advantage. Their work would not be hard; when their terms of transportation were over, they would be conveyed back to England, if they wished. Also, according to Bowes:

> "It was the Governor's pleasure that, if any partiality or reciprocal affection should take place between the male and female convicts going there, or after their arrival at New Norfolk, they might marry, and that he had authorized the surgeon, Mr Jamison, to perform that office and after a time the clergyman would be sent there to re-marry them."

Susan Gough only just made it. In fact, another convict — Anne

Yates — had been recommended as a very fit person to go — but she wished to continue where she was.

Why? I thought. What compelling power urged Anne Yates to remain at Port Jackson when she might have taken advantage of such a desirable offer?

It could only be romance! And sure enough, on the 16th March, 1788 — less than three months later, an entry appears in the official records as follows: —

> "Joseph Theakston was baptized. He was the son of Joseph Theakston, a marine, and of Anne Yates, a convict."

However, there appear to have been subsequent complications, for on the 14th November, 1791, there is yet another entry:

> "The daughter of David Collins and Anne Yeates (Yates) was christened Marrianne Letitia Collins."

The father of this, her second child, was none other than Captain David Collins, the Judge-Advocat. He already had a wife, Maria, back in England — but on the 15th January, 1791 she had written to him expressing her rather bitter dissatisfaction at their protracted separation. Could it be that she had heard something, some whisper of gossip from that lonely outpost at the other side of the world? Or was it just that any wife who could write in such vein to her husband in such circumstances was hardly worth bothering about anyway?

What happened to the other convicts who went to Norfolk Island? Of Elizabeth Lee, Elizabeth Hipsley, Elizabeth Colley and Olivia Gascoin there is no further news.

Ann Innett, however, had an affair with the Commandant at Norfolk Island, Lieutenant G. P. King. On the 9th July, 1790 their son was baptized Philip Gidley King. One supposes that, if you are a convict, the best person to have an affair with is the Commandant. It certainly worked well for Ann Innett. In the end she married Richard John Robinson, by special permission, on 18th November, 1792. Robinson was a convict. Eleven days after his marriage he received what must have seemed like a wedding gift from Governor Phillip. It was:

> "Absolute Remission of the Sentence of Transportation passed on Richard John Robinson (now employed at the Public Barn and Granaries at Parramatta) at the Expiration of Seven Years from the Fourth day of June, 1791."

I could find no subsequent mention in the official records of any of the male convicts who went to Norfolk Island, nor of Batchelor, Kerridge or Westbrook.

Roger Morley, the Master Weaver, however, did well. On the 14th July, 1790 he was referred to by Phillip in a letter to Grenville as one "who you are pleased to say shall be recommended for a suitable compensation, if brought forward in my contingent account." Again, on the 23rd March, 1791, Phillip wrote to Nepean concerning the services rendered by Mr Roger Morley.

                              *   *   *

So the *Supply* weighed anchor and made sail down the harbour at 6 p.m. on the 14th February, 1788. The six months provisions aboard "certainly included some sheep, hogs and poultry, seeds and plants, with tools and implements for cleansing and cultivating the ground."

They were quickly overtaken by a severe gale which continued until the 16th. No damage was done—but two days of battering under such circumstances must have weighed them down with a growing sense of responsibility. In the light of after events, if anything had happened to the little *Supply* on this voyage—then the First Settlement could hardly have survived at all.

On the 17th February, they discovered an island, but the wind was now fair and it was essential to push on and to fulfil the task upon which they were engaged. So they noted its position in the Log and they named it Lord Howe Island. A further examination of it could wait until they returned.

They eventually reached Norfolk Island on the 29th February (Leap Year's Day), but landing proved difficult. In fact, it was the 3rd March before any landing at all was effected as the coast consisted of cliffs and rocks on which the seas broke with great violence. It was decided that it would be impractical to attempt landing the stores and provisions there and David Blackburn was sent in charge of a long-boat to find a more suitable spot at the south end of the island.

He found such a place and to it King, with very little originality, gave the name of Sydney Bay. At this place, all the colony, with all their precious stores and provisions, were landed safely.

For six days, the crew of the *Supply* stayed there, supervising the settling-in process for the colony. Then, having seen the tents established and the stores under cover, they took leave of them all, boarded the gallant *Supply* and steered for their newly-discovered island.

It was the evening of the 9th March when they left.

On the 12th March, they anchored in a large bay on the south-west of Lord Howe Island and went ashore.

CHAPTER SEVEN

David Blackburn Writes Home

WHEN I began to write this book, I naturally looked for a "focal point" — some item of special human interest on which I hang the whole thing.

Scanning through the typewritten copies of the letters quickly, it did appear that there was some mystery about Blackburn's death and particularly about the long silence which preceded this event. No letters home. No news to his sister. Just silence. It seemed that this might well be looked into and, at first, I thought this would have to do. History by itself can be a dull dog that scarcely ever wags its tail. The cold, statistical record of events in retrospect needs the touch of humanity before it becomes readable by many people.

When I taught history to unfortunate children in a hot classroom on a summer's afternoon, I had every sympathy with the boy whose gaze wandered to the cool grass and the trees beyond the window. For facts are never enough. Indeed, history never consists of facts by themselves. It is made of warm flesh and blood, stirred up by aspiration and ambition, flavoured with triumph, tragedy and courage and served hot. The cold dish that we digest has lost much of its appeal and its only merit is that we now see the real importance of the suffering and striving that made the meal.

So I wanted a focal point. And there came a day when I took one letter in my hand, the four sheets covered with close and faded writing. And in that moment, this book came to life for me.

*　　*　　*

For a moment, however, it is 1973. Over two million people live in Sydney. The harbour bridge is one of the largest arch bridges in the world. The municipalities, Manly, Hunter's Hill, Bankstown and Botany are teeming with history in one of the major cities of the world. The forty million pound Sydney Opera House, the Australia Square Tower 550 feet high, the A.M.P. Building — these all look down on the everlasting port.

It is 1973. Last summer the Australians were fighting to regain the Ashes at Edgbaston, the Oval and Lords. At Munich, a large contingent of Australian athletes vied with the other nations of the world for Olympic honours, their efforts being watched by perhaps five hundred million people. An Australian, Shane Gould, won three gold medals. And later, another Australian, Belinda Green, became Miss World to the delight of most people who saw her — for they had got it right for once!

At the moment of writing, the population of this vast continent whose area, according to Whittaker's Almanac, has been judged to be 2,967,909 square miles (how on earth do they arrive at the odd 9?), must be over thirteen million people, the great majority of them Europeans.

*　　*　　*

I pick up this letter, struggle with the fading ink and get each word safely on to the dictaphone.

It is 1788 and David Blackburn is writing to his sister back in England.

Where is he sitting? Is he aboard the *Supply*? Is he reclining on some rock where the Opera House will one day be? He does not know the importance of his actions. He would be surprised to find the words he writes transformed to type, put into a book, preserved in some University for as long as history lasts.

But this is what history is all about. The daily actions of little people, most of them unknown; the thoughts and reflections of millions; the determination and uncertainties of the few; the courage of the many. These are the drops of water that form the ocean whose tide sweeps humanity onwards to its ultimate fulfilment.

It is Saturday, 12th July, 1788, a cloudy day with west to southwest winds. The temperature is 53°.

It seems to be a day for letter writing.

Governor Phillip wrote two letters.

The Reverend Mr Johnson wrote to Mr Ewen Nepean (Under Secretary to the Home Department).

Lieutenant Clark (a real old gossip if ever there was one!) wrote to B. Hartnell and to Lieutenant Reynolds.

Daniel Southwell, mate of the *Sirius,* wrote to his mother and to the Reverend Mr Butler.

John White, the Surgeon-General, wrote to Lord Sydney concerning the shortages in the colony.

Captain Campbell wrote a letter to Lord Ducie.

Mr Augustus Alt, the Surveyor-General, wrote to Lord Sydney.

And David Blackburn wrote two long letters, one to his friend Richard Knight, the other to his sister Margaret in Norwich.

There was, of course, a very good reason for all this frantic letter writing. Four transports were under orders for sailing to England.

It is possible, in some degree at least, to imagine the thoughts and feelings in the hearts of all the human beings who were living in New South Wales on that day. They had been there almost six months. They had been away from their homes for a year and two months. And any letters they sent — as they well knew — would not reach England for a further six months.

Supply — Sidney Cove.
Port Jackson 12th July, 1788.

> Miss Blackburn,
> St Michael's, Coslany,
> Norwich.

My dear Sister,

As I wrote to you from Teneriffe, Rio Janeiro and the Cape of Good Hope, which letters I hope you have received, I shall now give you a short account of our voyage from the Cape to the present time. We sailed from thence on the 13th of November. Met with contrary winds and sent on but slowly for the first week. The wind then came fair and on the 25th the Governor, a Lieut. King and Lieut. Dawes, came on board the Supply and we made all sail for New Holland, leaving the fleet to follow us under the care of H.M. Ship Sirius. We had a very quick but windy passage, and made Van Diemansland, the south part of New Holland, on the 3rd of January 1788, having run in 50 days the distance of very near 6000 miles. But it was the 19th before we arrived at Botany Bay, where we anchored at 4 in the afternoon, all in good health and on the 21st the rest of the fleet arrived. The next day, the Governor, Captain Hunter, the Master of the Sirius and myself, went to examine a place where Captain Cook supposed (to have landed) and there was a harbour to which he gave the name of Port Jackson. We found it an excellent and extensive one and on the 25th returned to Botany Bay and conducted the whole fleet up the harbour to the place where the camp and storehouses now stand. It is about 6 miles from the entrance. The Governor has named it Sidney Cove. In the beginning of February, we took on board six months' provisions, with the necessary implements for settling a colony on Norfolk Island, discovered by Captain Cook and on the 14th sailed with Lieut. King as Superintendent and Commandant of Norfolk Isle, a surgeon a midshipman, a master weaver, with 9 men and 6 women convicts. We were soon overtaken by a very severe gale of wind which continued till the 16th but did us no damage, and on the 17th we discovered an island, to which we gave the name of Lord Howe Island. As the wind continued fair, we put off an examination of this island till our return. We arrived at Norfolk Isle on the 29th of February but it was the 3rd of March before we were able to land, which we did with the utmost difficulty, but found it would be impossible to land the stores and provisions there as the sea broke with great violence on the shore. We therefore went in search of a better place which I discovered by going in a boat to the south end of the island where on the 6th and 7th we landed the colony with all their stores and provisions safe. To this place, Lieut. King gave the name of Sidney Bay.

This Colony is settled here with the idea of cultivating and improving the flax plant and cutting down fir trees with which the island is covered and grow to an amazing height and size. Some of them measured 27 feet round. This island is about 15 miles round. It is in general surrounded by inaccessible rocks and high perpendicular cliffs on which the sea breaks with such violence that landing is always difficult and very often impractible. Having seen the colony settled in their tents, on the 9th in the evening, took leave of them and now steered for our new discovered island which we made on the 12th, and anchored in the large bay on its south west side and at 4 in the afternoon displayed the English colours on shore and took formal possession of the island in the name of his Brittanic Majesty. Lieut. Ball then named the different parts of the island. It is about 6 miles long and about 2 wide. At its south east end are two very high mountains which he named Mount Gower and Mount Lidgbird, the valley between them Erskine Valley. There is one large bay and two small ones on its South west side. The two small ones he

43

called Callam Bay, the name of our surgeon, the other Hunter Bay after Captain John Hunter of the Sirius, the large bay Prince William Henry Bay and a small green island nearly in the middle of it Blackburn Isle. I was on board whilst this ceremony was performing, or it should have been called Knight Isle. The island is uninhabited but we found plenty of the finest turtle I ever saw on the beach, some of them weighing upwards of 500 pounds. The bays abound with excellent fish and the island with pigeons, a kind of quail and some other birds peculiar to the place. But no running stream of fresh water that we saw. We took on board as many turtle as we could conveniently stow and made sail for Port Jackson where we arrived on the 20th March. The turtle were an acceptable present to the Governor and colony. We have been since at Howe Island and are now preparing to sail with the fresh supply of stores and provisions for Norfolk Island. We really know so little of New South Wales that it is useless to attempt to describe it.

The Land in general is very rocky and small spaces of clear ground. Our gardens have produced nothing worth notice, nor I am afraid will not whilst we remain in the colony which I hope will not exceed two years. The natives are black, they are quite naked and very dirty and are to all appearances most miserable wretches—they live in caves and hollow places in the rocks and so far as we know have no other food but fish and fern root. They almost always go armed with spears, very long and barbed at the end with a fish bone. We have never yet been able to persuade them to come in to the camp or on board the ships, tho' they frequently pass and once three canoes came alongside the Supply but would not come in, nor will they eat or drink with us nor taste any of our food. They seem to be a harmless inoffensive people but like all savage nations are cunning and will always sooner or later revenge an injury. They have killed a convict and wounded another who were in the woods collecting herbs, but we have every reason to believe they were the agressors, indeed the convicts in general are a set of most abandoned wretches—four have been hanged for breaking into and robbing the officers' tents. We have never seen above 40 of the natives in a body but once. On the 6th of June, a party of gentlemen with their servants and 4 soldiers walking to Botany Bay met with a body of 300 of them all armed with spears and targets. However, they did not atempt to disturb our small party but let them quietly pass. On the 4th of June, His Majesty's birthday was kept here, the Sirius and Supply fired 21 cannon each at sun rise at noon and at sun set. All the officers of the Navy and Army dined with the Governor who then named the adjacent country round Port Jackson the County of Cumberland. On the 22nd of June at 20 minutes after 4 o'clock in the afternoon a shock of an earthquake was felt on board the ships and through the camp. Our surgeon and me were then in the woods about a mile and a half from the camp and were at that time standing still and silent examining some gum running from a large tree. The shock was an undulation from south west and did not continue I think more than two seconds of time. It was accompanied by a noise like a distant cannon. The trees shook as if a gale of wind was blowing. The afternoon was remarkably clear and a very light breeze at N.N.E. I have enjoyed very good health since we left England and I think this climate a very healthy one. There has been but 50 buried since our arrival here and as many marriages and 26 births. It is said that some ships will be sent to us next spring. If so I hope I shall hear from you and my friend Knight to whom I have wrote a fuller account of our voyage than I have time to do now.

I hope my good mother is well and that yourself and sister Elizabeth established in health and spirits. Perhaps you are still among our worthy friends at Newbury or Devizes and I hope you are because I know you must be happy there. I hope your Laetitia is in good health and happy. I beg you will make my love and respects to the family. My duty to my mother, love to Eliza, brother and little niece and respects to our friends at Norwich. Adieu my dear sister and believe me your ever affectionate

brother
D. Blackburn

This letter, of course, is very much a piece of history, and all of it is important. But as I read it through slowly and carefully, a few brief sentences leapt into life for me:

"…Having seen the colony settled in their tents, on the 9th in the evening, took leave of them and now steered for our new discovered island which we made on the 12th, and anchored in the large bay on its south west side and at 4 in the afternoon displayed the English colours on shore and took formal possession of the island in the name of his Brittanic Majesty. Lieut. Ball then named the different parts of the island. It is about six miles long and about 2 wide. At its south-east end are two very high mountains which he named Mount Gower and Mount Lidgbird, the valley between them Erskine Valley. There is one large bay and two small ones on its south west side. The two small ones he called Callam Bay, the name of our surgeon, the other Hunter Bay after Captain John Hunter of the Sirius, the large Bay Prince William Henry Bay *and a small green island nearly in the middle of it Blackburn Isle.*"

CHAPTER EIGHT

The Island is Lost

I PUT the letter down and found myself sitting very still. In the quietude of my study, it seemed as though the curtains of Time had been pulled aside. This letter, this very piece of paper, had been handled by the man whose little green island endured in the Pacific Ocean. I saw the *Supply* sailing in there, anchoring in a bay as yet un-named. I saw the long-boat launched and the party go ashore. I sensed the excitement of that bright afternoon, as they walked among the turtles and the strange birds — utterly unafraid of visitors because man had never set foot there before.

A few minutes later, I got the car out of the garage and started on my way to Norwich.

*　　*　　*

It was a journey of some fifteen miles and the roads were quiet enough for reflection. Perhaps it was as well, for certainly my mind was still back in the eighteenth century. A curious two-dimensional experience was happening to me. These tree-lined roads of sun and shadow were removed by time and space from all that I was concerned with. Thirteen thousand miles of space. Nearly two hundred years of time. Yet it was the same sun that had shone down on them during that March afternoon. It was David Blackburn's pen and his hand that drove me now towards the City of Norwich so that I might look at his island. There was no separation. Life was a continuity.

*　　*　　*

I parked the car outside the splendid City Library and went to my usual place in the Reference Room. Within minutes I was looking at photographs of Mount Gower and Mount Lidgbird and reading useful information about Lord Howe Island, excitement mounting within me all the time. Blackburn had been slightly out in his estimation of its size. It was not six miles by two. It was seven miles by three. However, all that could wait. First, I must find Blackburn Island.

Now our Norwich City Library is not merely a fine building. It is also one of the best Libraries in the country. Its Staff are always helpful, the Librarian himself has achieved a fine reputation in his field. It had a fair stock of reference books about Australasia and I knew where to look. So I looked. And I looked. But in vain.

No matter where I searched, I could find no mention of it. No Australian encyclopaedia had heard of it. Spate, Lee, Thompson, Griffith Taylor, Laborde, Henry Rees—none of them had heard of it. No index showed it.

The glow that had enveloped me all afternoon disappeared. I felt deflated, temporarily defeated. I felt like a child whose special treat had been postponed by a sudden downpour of rain.

But, unless it had sunk, the island must be still there. And before I left the Library, I took the opportunity of noting one or two useful facts.

It appeared that Lord Howe Island was considered part of New South Wales—a natural enough consequence—since New South Wales was all there was in those days. It was administered by a special Board called The Lord Howe Island Administration Board whose offices were located in Sydney. Armed with this information, I found my car and drove back to Itteringham.

*　　*　　*

The next day I sent a letter by air to Sydney, asking for any helpful literature concerning Lord Howe Island and in particular a map of that area showing any small adjacent islands.

It was November when I wrote. It was to be late January before any news came. For Australia, even by air, is still a long way away.

CHAPTER NINE

Lord Howe and Norfolk Islands

S O I had to wait. I am an impatient person and I did not enjoy
waiting. I must have been unbearable to live with, but fortunately
I had much to get on with.

Since I had to wait, it is only fair that readers should wait too, and
this seems the appropriate moment for a look at both Lord Howe
Island and also Norfolk Island.

Lord Howe Island is a crescent-shaped island 436 miles north-east
of Sydney. Its Latitude is 31 30S. Its Longitude is 159 5E. It was
named after Richard Howe, the famous British Admiral.

It measures 7 miles by 3 miles (not 6 × 2 as mentioned by
David Blackburn). No traces have been found of any previous
occupation by human beings.

The following note is quoted from *Australia* (Griffith Taylor,
1940):

"It was early visited by whalers who killed off certain rare birds.
The first Settlement was in 1834. The early settlers cultivated
maize, potatoes and onions, and the latter are exported. In 1869
there were 35 folk living on the island, and in 1954 the population
was 278. (The *permanent* population however, in 1954 was only
136 according to another source..)

The island is covered with thick vegetation, in which there are
several beautiful genera of palms and tree-ferns. The top of Mount
Gower is a veritable botanical museum, as several species of fern
and moss are not found anywhere else in the world. There are 207
species of plant, of which 56 are endemic. The plants are akin to
those found in Australia, but the shells seem to link it with New
Zealand. Porphyria, a flightless bird, has vanished, and is only
known from one skin in the Vienna Museum. The chief article of
export is the seed of a dwarf palm (Kentia or Howea) of which as

49

much as 4000 bushels a year are sold to horticulturists all over the world."

The 1939-45 war brought about a change in the industry of the island, for it is now a place of refuge for tourists who seek its beauty and peace. The tourist industry is, in fact, its main source of revenue, and the islanders, whose general business consists of agriculture and fishing, now cater more and more for visitors. There is a flying-boat service twice weekly from Sydney, and the island has a weather reporting station.

Geologists believe that both Lord Howe Island and Norfolk Island were once part of the New Zealand volcanic land-mass to which they are connected by deep sunken banks.

After its discovery Lord Howe Island was neglected for many years, the main reason being probably lack of a good anchorage.

The first attempt at settlement was in 1834 by three white men from New Zealand. This group, however, was bought out by Poole and Dawson (an ironmonger). Dawson eventually left and Poole ruled the island. By 1851 there were sixteen who were self-subsistent. They lived by exporting the Kentia palm seed and by supplying provisions to whalers. By 1900 there were one hundred people living on the island.

Lord Howe Island is well known by both botanists and ornithologists. Over one hundred species of birds have been recorded. Unfortunately, the fact that they knew no fear of human beings was the downfall of many of them. They had been alone for centuries, and were exceptionally tame. One can imagine what happened when the whalers visited the island. At least eight of the original species are now extinct.

Reading over the above it seems a dreadful thing that I should have had to write that sentence:

"The fact that they knew no fear of human beings was the downfall of many of them."

We are the superior race on this planet. We have more intelligence than any other species. We have more gifts and more power.

It is time we had more compassion for the other creatures we hold to be inferior.

For we neglect such considerations at our own peril. Our callousness makes us lower than any animals we ever slaughter.

The *Geographical Magazine* for January, 1958, published a most interesting account of Lord Howe Island by Mary de Bunsen and have kindly given me permission to quote from it.

Mary de Bunsen first heard about Lord Howe Island when she read a book by Francis Chichester who had rebuilt his damaged Moth seaplane there in the course of a trans-Tasman Sea flight. Twenty years later, she spent six months on Lord Howe and was able to see the changes that had taken place.

Way back in the eighteenth century, Surgeon Bowes of the *Lady Penrhyn* (one of the nine Transports with the First Fleet, a ship of 331 tons) wrote of Lord Howe:

"When I was in the woods amongst the Birds I could not help picturing to myself the Golden Age as described by Ovid — to see the Fowls or Coots some white, some blue and white, others all blue with large red bills and a patch of red on top of their heads and the Boobies in thousands...walking totally fearless and unconcerned in all parts around us."

Mary de Bunsen writes:
"Lord Howe Island has been more or less accessible since the days of the Australian gold rush, when sixty or eighty ships a year called there *to provision*..."

The italics are mine — for the words "to provision" conjures up a dreadful picture for me. What was there in the way of provisions in that lonely place apart from turtles and birds?

The article goes on:
"The earliest settlers, round about the 1840s, began the slaughter which has left few landbirds on the island. However, they did a useful job supplying ships, for it was risky to provision at Sydney, where whole crews would desert and make their way to the gold-fields. Local whaling contributed to this artificial boom, but when it subsided, visiting ships diminished to one or two a year and the islanders settled down to subsistence farming.

Once a year, on a fixed day in March, most of the islanders knock off work and start to pick palm-seeds, the season lasting until September. The first schoolmaster, an Englishman called Thomas Bryant Wilson (who also brought over the first Norfolk Island pines), discovered that the indigenous palm (formerly *Kentia* and now called *Howea Forsteriana*) grew well in cool climates. In fact it is the palm you still see in old-fashioned hotels in England. He founded the socialized palm-seed industry which brought the islanders a steady livelihood until World War II. But the quantity exported had fallen from 2500 to about 300 bushels a year when in 1947 the aeroplanes came and brought the tourists with them. Even so, the accumulated funds from this industry still enable the island to be administered without a government grant.

We only stayed six months on Lord Howe Island, but I have thought a lot about it since we left. An island like this, not too cut off, is a microcosm of advancing civilization. The penalties show up clearly: loss of health and stamina from too-civilized food; increasing worry about making money to buy higher education and consumer goods (not, thank goodness, to 'keep up with the Joneses') and the epidemics that tourists bring, though these follow the same world pattern and are giving way to medical science while degenerative disease is on the increase. Nevertheless, half the island went down with the same type of influenza that was ravaging Australia. To these draw-backs one may add a weekly fever to write all the letters that have been left until the last minute before the flying-boat arrives. But it is a good life still, for those who have the inner resources to live it to the full, and many of the islanders ask for nothing better."

Of course, Mary de Bunsen wrote her article during or before 1958. Nowadays, I believe, Lord Howe Island is fairly widely advertised in eastern Australia as a tourist centre. I myself am not one who believes that civilisation is such an evil thing in itself. I know all the facile arguments about old ways of life being destroyed, and the easy-going habits of people being disrupted. But there is another side to the coin. The old ways are not all harmony — and never have been. (It was well over a hundred and fifty years ago that they were destroying the birds on Lord Howe, remember!) And the new ways — though they may bring some abuse in their train — being a wider life to people who have a right to the same opportunities as all of us. There is no reason at all why Lord Howe Island, during the next few decades should not become a prosperous tourist centre, offering both peace and beauty to many who want to escape from the pressures of Sydney — less than three hours flying-time away. A wise administration could see real progress and real preservation march hand in hand.

*   *   *

With regard to Norfolk Island, this had been first discovered by Captain James Cook on the 10th October 1774. When the little

Supply landed its settlers in March 1788, it became the second oldest British settlement in the Pacific Ocean.

The settlement continued until 1813 when all the inhabitants were transferred to "New Norfolk" in Tasmania.

The penal settlement was re-established in 1825. It continued until 1856 when the Island was abandoned to make way for the descendants of the *Bounty* mutineers who landed there from Pitcairn Island on the 8th June 1856.

In July 1914 the Commonwealth Government took over the administration of Norfolk Island as an "external territory".

*   *   *

But to go back to its beginnings, it will be remembered that the First Fleet arrived at Botany Bay on the 18th January, 1788. The fact that Lieutenant King was appointed as Governor at Norfolk Island as early as 30th January—a mere twelve days later—shows that this region must have been well in the forefront of Governor Phillip's mind.

The instructions received by Philip Gidley King with his Commission were to superintend and command a settlement to be formed there; to proceed thence in the armed tender *Supply* with men, women, stores and provisions and, after taking all necessary measures to receiving same, to proceed immediately to the cultivation of the flax plant (which grew spontaneously on the island), cotton, corn and other grains. He was given seeds of the latter items, but was urged to use only such part of the corn raised as might be found necessary.

He was urged to keep an exact account of the increase of any crops which would be disposed of by the Crown. He was furnished with provisions for six months and was asked to make these last as long as possible.

A great deal of attention was given in these instructions to the necessity for keeping Norfolk Island safe against any interpolaters and extreme precautions were also to be taken against the possibility of any escape by the convicts by boat.

"You will be furnished with a four-oared boat, and you are not on any consideration to build or to permit the building of any vessel or boat whatever that is decked, or of any boat or vessel that is not decked, whose length or keel exceeds twenty feet; and if by accident any vessel or boat that exceeds twenty feet should be driven on the island, you are immediately to cause such boat or vessel to be scuttled or otherwise rendered unserviceable, letting her remain in that state until you receive further directions from me."

Also:

"You are not to permit any intercourse or trade with any ships or vessels that may stop at the island, whether English or of any other Nation, unless such ships or vessels are in distress, in which case you are to afford them such assistance as may be in your power."

In a letter to Mr Henry Fricker dated 15th November, 1788, Johnson wrote from Sidney Cove:

"The Colony begins already to be a good deal dispersed. About 70 or 80 are gone to settle in New Norfolk — this took place soon after our arrival — ships have been backward and forward — and the last particularly brings us a flattering promising account of that Island as to wood — Garden Stuff etc."

This account was brought back to Sydney by David Blackburn commanding the *Golden Grove*.

On 17th November, 1788 Phillip, in a letter to Nepean, referred to flax from Norfolk Island which he was forwarding to England.

The *Supply* sailed again for Norfolk Island on 17th February, 1789 with 21 male convicts, 6 female convicts and three children. Two of the children, a boy (3) and a girl (4) were put under the care of Lieutenant King. They were to be instructed in reading and writing and husbandry and five acres of ground were to be cultivated for their benefit — rather a large allocation, one would have thought, bearing in mind the needs of the colony as a whole.

On the 24th March, 1789 the *Supply* arrived at Sydney Cove from Norfolk Island bringing news of an attempted mutiny there. On board the ship was the alleged ringleader William Francis. I cannot find anywhere details of his trial — but he certainly survived for his marriage to Mary Jones is recorded on Christmas Day, 1790. On this occasion the *Supply* brought into Port Jackson three turtles from Lord Howe Island.

On 6th November, 1789, there was a reduction of one-third of the rations for the whole population of Norfolk Island—from the Governor to the convicts by order of Phillip.

The *Supply* returned from Norfolk Island on 21st December with very favourable reports of the corn, and with a cask of flax seeds in pod.

By this time the convict population of Norfolk Island was steadily on the increase. Every visiting ship took more. On the 7th January, 1790, the *Supply* sailed with 22 male and two female convicts, and one child. It is worthy of note that in the third year of the first settlement (1790) there were 591 persons at Sydney and no less than 418 on Norfolk Island. At the end of 1791 (after the arrival of the Second Fleet with its terrible consignment of convicts in a most pitiable state) the population of Norfolk Island rose to 1172. No doubt one of the main reasons for this dramatic increase lay in the fact that escape on the mainland was fairly easy. The consequences were often dire—but freedom was a temptation too great to be resisted. Such escapes led to bush-ranging.

From Norfolk Island, no such escapes were possible and in time it became a place of dread for many convicts. An official's wife, writing of the early years there, says:

"During the twelve months we were in the island 109 were shot by the sentries in self-defence, and 62 bayoneted to death, whilst the average number of lashes administered every day was 600."

On the 6th March, 1790 both the *Sirius* and the *Supply* sailed for Norfolk Island. Oddly enough, Phillip had written to Lieutenant King but five days before paying tribute to his services as Lieutenant Governor and in this letter there is a curious note of prescience:

"A full proportion of the provisions we have are sent with them, after deducting what may be necessary to send the *Supply* to the Cape, *if the* Sirius *should meet with any accident...*"

There were 161 convicts and 25 children on the *Sirius* and 22 convicts and three children on the *Supply*.

One month later on the 5th April, the *Supply* returned alone with the news that the *Sirius* had been lost. Fortunately every person aboard had been saved. But this was grievous news—especially since it was not known at first whether the provisions could be saved.

That evening there was an emergency meeting at Government House, when Phillip explained to everybody the now desperate state of the colony. Several important decisions were taken. All private boats were called in for the purpose of fishing and an officer was appointed as Fishing Superintendent. The Gamekeepers were to kill kangaroos for the public and severe rationing was imposed. The *Supply* was to be sent to Batavia for provisions and her Commander was ordered to charter a ship to bring further supplies.

David Blackburn, as will be seen from his subsequent letters, was present on all these occasions. He saw the *Sirius* wrecked. He was probably at the Government House meeting. And he went with the *Supply* to Batavia.

A young man whose name is unknown, writing home from Port Jackson at that time, said:

"I seize this opportunity of letting you know by a vessel that will sail very soon, our wretched situation, which has been occasioned by the miscarriage of our supplies. To give a just description of the hardships that the meanest of us endure, and the anxieties suffered by the rest, is more than I can pretend to. In all the Crusoe-like adventures I ever read or heard of, I do not recollect anything like it."

David Blackburn made at least three voyages to Norfolk Island.

The first was on the 14th February, 1788 when he sailed under King. Returned to Port Jackson 20th March.

The second was on the 2nd October, 1788 when he was in command of *The Golden Grove*. The log of *The Golden Grove* has the entry:

"Came on board from H.M. Ship *Sirius* one corporal and 5 mariners with a sergeant from the garrison with 21 men convicts 11 women do., and 3 free people for Norfolk Island. Likewise Mr Blackburn and 4 seamen and *Supply* jolly boat to assist in landing at Norfolk."

The following is the directive by Phillip, the original of which I have before me painstakingly written out by David Collins and signed by Phillip. This document is referred to in the official record, dated 27th September 1788, thus:

"*The Golden Grove* received an order from the Governor to proceed to Norfolk Island, under the direction of Mr Blackburne, Master of the *Supply.*"

By his Excellency Arthur Phillip Esq Governor in Chief and

Captain General, in and over His Majesty's territory of New South Wales and its Dependancies, and Captain of His Majesty's Ship *Sirius* —

You are hereby required and directed to go on board The Golden Grove, Store Ship (the Master having my order to follow your directions) and proceed with the said Ship to Norfolk Island. When you will land the people, Stores and Provisions, put on board for that purpose, and of which a particular account will be given you by His Majesty's Commissary for this settlement. And having so done you are to receive on board such spars and deals as the Commandant of the Island may be able to put on board with which you are to return to this port, without further loss of time.

Given under my hand, at Headquarters,
Port Jackson, New South Wales, this 25th September, 1788.

(signed) A. Phillip

Mr David Blackburn,
Master of His Majesty's
    Armed Tender,
        Supply
    by Command of His Excellency
        David Collins, Secretary.

The third was on the 22nd June, 1791 when he was in command of the *Supply*. On that day Collins wrote that the *Supply* sailed for Norfolk Island,

"...having some provisions on board for that settlement. She was to bring back Captain Hunter, with the officers and crew of His Majesty's late ship *Sirius*. Her Commander, Lieutenant Ball, labouring under a very severe and alarming disposition, Mr David Blackburn, the Master, was directed by the Governor to take charge of her until Mr Ball should be able to resume the command. He returned 26th February, 1791."

CHAPTER TEN

The Strange Silence

IN NOVEMBER 1788 — on the 15th day to be exact — Blackburn wrote a long letter to his sister Margaret from Sydney Cove.

It was an historic letter, the full text of which is given in the Appendix, and it contained an interesting account of the natives, kangaroos, and even a false report of a gold mine.

At this time, the first crops had been sown.

"There is now some wheat and barley which promises to do well, if the small animals of the oppossum kind and the ants (of both which here are great numbers) do not destroy it. The valleys abound with cabbage trees with which most of the houses are built for the present and several stone buildings are begun. The Governor's house will be a very elegant one and is near finished."

Less than two hundred years later, Brian Kennedy wrote:

"The period of less than two hundred years between the first and the latest of the Wentworths has seen Sydney grow from a convict settlement to a dynamic city. Her people continue to buy more cars and better washing machines, with only an occasional glance at South-East Asia. Planners estimate that by the end of the century Sydney will have five million people. The City will stretch from Newcastle, now one hundred miles to the north, to Wollongong, now fifty miles to the south.

This suburban city is already a suburb of the world rather than an isolated outpost. London is twenty-seven hours away by jet, and San Francisco fourteen hours. By 1971 the supersonic Concorde will have cut the flying time to London to thirteen hours twenty minutes, and the time to San Francisco to seven hours thirty-five minutes. Perhaps by the end of the century Sydney's urban sprawl will simply have merged with one gigantic suburb covering the globe."

In the latter part of this letter, Blackburn describes Norfolk Island. "A beautiful spot" he writes, "and bids fair to be a valuable acquisition to the Government."

He goes on, however,

"It is much to be regretted that this island affords no harbour or place of safety for ships and that landing is almost always attended with great difficulty and danger on account of the violence with which the sea dashes against the shore which in general is steep and rocky. A midshipman and four men were drowned in a boat the last time we were there in the Supply, though the sea was then apparently smooth."

In this regard, it should be noted that it was David Blackburn, above all others, who was responsible for the safety of ships and personnel arriving at Norfolk Island. His letter to King (dated 13th October, 1788) shows the extent and method of his work in this regard. And it must also be remembered that it was Blackburn who, in charge of a long-boat, discovered the best landing place at Sydney Bay at the south end of the island. The subsequent wreck of the *Sirius* on the 19th March, 1790 was in no way his responsibility. He was nowhere near the scene of the disaster. Indeed, if more notice had, in fact, been taken of his earlier findings, perhaps this tragedy might never have happened.

*   *   *

There now comes a strange interlude in the correspondence from Blackburn. The letter mentioned above would not have arrived in England until some time after May, 1789. From then on there is a very long and almost inexplicable silence.

Back in Norwich, Blackburn's mother and sister are clearly very worried.

An indication of their concern may be gathered from a letter signed by Mrs Blackburn's nephew, Peter Martineau, and dated London, 10th February, 1791. It reads as follows:

TO: FROM:
Mrs Blackburn,   Nephew Peter Martineau
Magdalen Street,   London, 10th Feb., 1791.
Norwich.

Dear Madam,
Lieutenant King, whom I had the pleasure this morning of meeting at his appartments, though an extreme polite civil man, yet he was not so communicative as I could have wished, for immediately upon hearing my business, he proposed giving me a few lines that would say everything he knew relative to Mr

Blackburn; this I conceived as meant to put a stop to any further enquiries I might be about making. He, however, spoke in the highest possible terms of esteem and friendship of my cousin David, and the sickness which he mentions he is just recovering from was a rheumatic complaint but that he was much better when he saw him than he had been for two or three months before.

The reason for his not writing he can by no means account for, he says it is particularly strange as most likely it will be six months before you can hear again.

I wish it had been in my power to have given you a more satisfactory account. I shall always be happy to render you any service.

> With love to my cousins, believe me,
> > Your affectionate nephew,
> > > Peter Martineau.

My wife desires her affectionate remembrance.

The Lieutenant King that Peter Martineau saw that morning was, of course, the same Lieutenant Philip Gidley King, at first Aide de Camp to Phillip, then Governor of Norfolk Island — and later destined to become Governor of New South Wales.

How did he come to be at his apartment in London?

We find that he was given despatches for the Secretary of State and for the Admiralty in Sydney Cove on 17th April, 1790, ordered to embark on the *Supply* bound for Batavia.

"...from whence I was to make the best of my way to England with the above despatches, and Lieutenant Ball having received his Orders, I took leave of His Excellency and at Noon we sailed, with the wind at south-west carrying with us the fervent prayers of those we left behind for our safety. At 1 in the p.m. we were abreast of the heads of the Entrance of Port Jackson; and at Sunset it bore west-south-west 15 miles."

King returned to Port Jackson on the *Gorgon* arriving there on 21st September, 1791.

There is one other interesting sidelight here. We are apt to complain if our letters take a day or two longer to reach their destinations than they ought. But at the very time that Peter Martineau was anxiously interviewing Lieutenant King — a letter was no doubt already on its way. Because it had missed the ship carrying Lieutenant King to London, it probably would not have arrived until well into the summer of 1791.

Twenty months had elapsed since he wrote his last letter and, because he had missed the post, a further six months would have passed before it was received in England.

The writer of this letter, Peter Martineau, was David Blackburn's cousin and a brother of the famous Norwich Surgeon, Philip Meadows Martineau, who, at that time, would have been thirty-nine years of age.

P. M. Martineau was undoubtedly one of the more prominent citizens of Norwich. He became Senior Surgeon to the Norfolk and Norwich Hospital and upon his retirement due to ill-health he was made Honorary Consulting Surgeon. A splendid professional memoir of P. M. Martineau was published in 1831 and is to be found in The Norfolk and Norwich Library of which he was the joint founder — if not the actual founder himself. The following extract is taken from these Memoirs:

"In 1784 he conceived the plan of founding a Public Library at Norwich, and having consulted the leading persons of the City he called a meeting in St. Andrew's Hall, at which Robert Partridge, Esq., the Mayor, presided, and the result of which was the establishment of the present library. The Reverent John Peele, his fellow labourer in this excellent work, was the first president, and Mr Martineau the first vice-president. There are at this time six hundred permanent subscribers to the library, which contains (including the City library) upwards of nine thousand volumes, and its annual expenditure in the purchase of books amounts to between four and five hundred pounds."

It is in this library that I am sitting writing this today. The best part of two hundred years have passed since P. M. Martineau conceived the idea. Now it has 37,000 volumes and during its own history it has given help to, and received help from, the most brilliant and cultured of Norwich citizens — including such names as the Gurneys, Crome, Cotman, Borrow, the Rider Haggards, Augustine Birrell and R. H. Mottram.

*   *   *

The strange silence on the part of Blackburn over a period of twenty months, coupled with the curious behaviour of Lieutenant King when he was interviewed in London by Martineau, left me wondering.

What had happened out there on the other side of the world? What was the mystery—for mystery there certainly was—that caused such a man to stop writing home? It was not a matter of letters being written and afterwards being lost. Blackburn himself, writing again in 1790, admits that "it is now 20 months since I wrote to you." And his sister Margaret, to whom this was addressed, is beside herself with anxiety. In fact, she never recovered from it, and became quite obsessed with the idea that there was some sinister reason behind her brother's reticence.

I have gone into this matter as thoroughly as possible and have reached the conclusion that, while there is no proof of any kind as to a particular incident, there are nevertheless curiosities—mainly of omission—connected with the situation.

On the 7th day of April, 1788 David Blackburn had been Master of H.M. *Supply* for one year.

Accordingly, he received a certificate to that effect as follows:

These are to certify the Principal Officers and Commissioners of H.M. Navy that Mr. David Blackburn served as Master on board H.M. Armed Tender Supply under my command from the 8th day of April 1787 to the 7th day of April 1788 during which time he complied with the general printed instructions and was always sober and obedient and never six weeks absent from duty.

Given under my hand on board H.M. Armed Tender Supply
Sidney Cove, Port Jackson
New South Wales
7th day of April, 1788
(sgd.) H. L. BALL.

*   *   *

When I first saw this certificate written by Lieutenant H. L. Ball in his own hand, I thought maybe I had discovered the origins of our tax year. But it was mere coincidence. Blackburn took up his actual post on the 8th April and he was to get such a Certificate every year, as a matter of routine.

There is, however, one very curious fact which is worthy of note.

Among the original papers that I have been handling there are Certificates for the years 1787/8, 1788/9 and 1791/2.

These three Certificates are almost identical in their wording. Just the dates are different. They all say the same thing.

However, on the 15th day of May, 1792 a further Certificate is issued. It covers merely the period 8th April to 15th May and it is as follows:

These are to certify the Principal Officers and Commissioners of H.M. Navy that Mr David Blackburn served as Master of H.M. Armed Tender Supply under my command from the 8th day of April, 1792, to the date hereof, during which time he complied with the general printed instructions, was always sober and obedient to command and has not been six weeks absent either by sickness or any other occasion and has had no opportunity of making remarks the said Armed Tender having been for the most part in port.

Given under my hand on board H.M. Armed Tender Supply
this 15th day of May, 1792,
(sgd.) H. L. BALL.

The phrase "and has had no opportunity of making remarks" clearly means that Blackburn had had no opportunity of surveying points of interest, charting, etc. But why was a further Certificate needed to cover those five weeks? It had never been done before. Why should it be necessary now?

He was certainly not in bad odour with the Governor, for the following is an extract from Phillip to Mr Stephens dated Sydney, 18th November, 1791.

"The very business like conduct of Mr David Blackburn as Master of the Supply and during the time he commanded that vessel while Lieut Ball was sick on shore make it a duty incumbent upon me to point him out as an officer deserving of their Lordships' notice."

So why was notice, in fact, not taken of this important commendation? For over three years after Phillip had written—no action of any sort had been taken by the Admiralty that I can discover. And by that time Blackburn was dead.

The First Settlement was, of course, a hotbed of gossip and dissension and even if we allow for the strain put upon men under difficult circumstances, there is one name that stands out above all others as a mischief maker. It was Major Ross, the Commandant of Marines. He was clearly a most objectionable character and there is ample evidence to substantiate such a viewpoint. Here are a few — chosen almost at random from the official records.

1. *11th September, 1788.* Ross brings William Strong and a Richard Knight to Court Martial over a matter which was clearly far from any dereliction of duty, accusing them of having refused to allow his messenger to remove certain rafters from the saw-pit. At the hearing, it was made very clear that they had not refused. They had merely suggested that the rafters should be taken from the next pit where they were easily obtainable, as they themselves had had no authorization from Captain Tench. These two men were found not guilty and were acquitted.

But Major Ross is not satisfied. He insists that the Court meets again to reconsider its decision. The findings were: "The Court... having, with the most mature and strict deliberation, reconsidered the whole of the proceedings, find no cause to alter their original opinion."

2. These findings lead to a serious difference of opinion between Ross and Tench. In a strong letter to Stephens, Secretary of the Admiralty Board, Ross goes so far as to say: "I hope they (their Lordships) will not wonder at my entreating that their Lordships will please to order him to be recalled...as I have some doubt whether he can be tried for any other crime until his first offence has been tried. I have not, therefore, reported him to the Governor, or I would most assuredly have had him tried on a charge of disobedience of orders, neglect of duty, and contempt to his commanding officer."

I think we could well underline those last five words. That Tench had contempt for Major Ross is fairly certain. It was something that he must have shared with a great number of his colleagues.

3. Even Captain Campbell who seems to have supported Ross on varying occasions does not find lasting friendship with this arrogant, obstinate and over-bearing personality to be possible.

Clark wrote: "Ross and Campbell quarrelled and carried matters to such a height that they parted messes, and pass each other without speaking, except on duty..."

4. In a letter written to Mr Phillip Stephens, Secretary of the

Admiralty Board, Major Ross makes it abundantly plain that his relationship with Governor Phillip is cold in the extreme.

5. On 18th March, 1788, there was a Court Martial at which a Marine, Joseph Hunt, was tried for striking another man. He was found guilty. He was sentenced to ask William Dempsey's pardon publicly before the battalion or to receive one hundred lashes, surely a sensible decision—bearing in mind the situation of the garrison far from home and its future well-being.

This sentence infuriated Major Ross who was dissatisfied because the prisoner had a choice of sentence.

He instructed the Court to impose one sentence. The Court refused. They were again ordered by Ross. They again refused—five officers in all.

Major Ross then suspended these officers from all duties and placed them under arrest.

In a letter to the Governor these five (of whom Captain Tench, we may be sure, was one!) wrote:

"We conceive the treatment we have received so violent, and our present disgraceful situation so notorious, that we cannot, without injustice to our feelings, consent to have the arrest we now suffer under taken off until a public reparation should have been made for the indignity we have been used with."

Major Ross wrote to the Governor, looking for support—but after some correspondence was ordered to release the arrested men and to return them to duty.

6. There was a duel fought between Major Ross and Captain Hill on the 12th December, 1791. The cause of it is unknown—but men do not fight duels—especially men whose own lives are at risk in an unknown land—unless there is extreme bitterness between them. Add to this the fact that Captain Hill emerges from the story of the first settlement as a man of considerable compassion—and it is reasonable to suppose that Ross would have been at fault.

Now both Blackburn and Hill sailed for Norfolk Island on 22nd January, 1791. (Ross was already there).

Ross returned from Norfolk Island on 5th December, 1791.

Ross and Hill fight a duel on 12th December, 1791.

All these dates are very significant.

Even one of the convicts—a man named Francis Fowkes of Norfolk Island—wrote a letter some time towards the end of 1790 complaining of the conduct of Major Ross. He addressed it to the Judge Advocat, Captain David Collins. One might, at first, think nothing of a mere convict complaining. But we must bear in mind that it needed a great deal of courage on the part of such a person — for he would have been running grave risks to himself in the very act of making such a complaint. This convict married Susannah Bray, another convict, on 21st October, 1792.

7. In his introduction to the volume *Sydney Cove 1791 to 1792*, Doctor Cobley writes:

"The administrative difficulties caused by the unco-operative attitude of Major Ross, Commandant of Marines and Lieutenant Governor, were solved by transferring him to command this detachment. (Norfolk Island)"

8. Captain Campbell, writing to Lieutenant Clark at Norfolk Island, says on 6th August, 1791:

"This gentleman (Major Ross) I have ever found too much a time-server and too much attached to self-interest to have any high opinion of, or to repose more confidence in, than I would in any other character here."

9. Kylie Tennant, in *Australia — Her Story*, is much more forthright. She writes as follows:

"The news (of the French Revolution) must have shocked to the soul men who were accustomed to hang anyone who stole a morsel of bread, particularly men like Major Ross who took such a vicious delight in flogging the prisoners and insulting the Governor that Phillip finally sent him off to Norfolk Island with the worst of the convicts. There he could flog men to death but he could deliver complaints and insults only by letter."

But perhaps the most illuminating reference of all to the character of Ross is made in a letter from *Captain David Collins*, the Judge Advocate, to his *father* on 23rd March, 1791. He wrote as follows:

"Of my situation I will say this much — I still live with the Governor, and continue to be his Secretary. Since Major Ross went from hence, tranquility may be said to have been our guest, but whenever he returns Discord will again drive out Tranquility. Oh! that the 'Sirius' when she was lost, had proved his — but no more of that. While here, he made me the object of his persecution — and a Day will come — a Day of Retribution."

These are strong words indeed. They supply indisputable proof—
and there is much more that could be included—of the fact that
Major Ross was a bully of the worst possible kind—a man who was
determined to let no other stand in his way. His opinion of the new
settlement was about as low as it could be. His prophecies concerning
the future of New South Wales were short-sighted in the extreme
and differed from Governor Phillip's view as chalk differs from
cheese. His relationship with the men under his command was
fraught with all kinds of dissension.

During four years of service David Blackburn must have crossed
swords with him. It would have been impossible for it to be
otherwise.

Campbell, Clark, Hill, Collins, Tench, various officers of the
Marine Corps—even Governor Phillip himself—all of these saw Ross
for what he was—a bully of the worst kind. It is inconceivable to me
that David Blackburn, cooped aboard a little ship with this man on
a nine-hundred mile journey and living in the same settlement with
him for the best part of three years, should have escaped his
attentions. For Blackburn was a quiet, modest man whose main
concern seems to have been the performance of his duty. His nature
was such that it would have invited the attentions of the arrogant
and intolerant Major Ross.

Perhaps, somewhere under the surface of their relationship lies
the solution to the strange silence of a man who, though devoted to
his far-distant home, wrote no letters for twenty months. Perhaps
even the lack of promotion after Governor Phillip's warm com-
mendations could even be traced to Major Ross's interference.
Perhaps it was fear of Ross that accounted for Lieutenant King's
strange behaviour in his London apartments when confronted by
Martineau. Perhaps the niggling worries and frustrations of life in
the First Settlement, resulting in the deterioration of his health and
his death of consumption in 1795 might have been considerably less
but for this ogre of a man of whom Captain David Collins had
written:

"Whenever he returns Discord will drive out Tranquility. Oh—
that the Sirius when she was lost, had proved his—but no more of
that. While here, he made me the object of his persecution—
and the Day will come—a Day of Retribution."

Perhaps. That is all that can be said. Perhaps. It is unlikely that
history will ever unfold for us the truth.

67

CHAPTER ELEVEN

The Map Arrives—
And the Island is Found

ON THE 11th January, when I came down to breakfast, there was a large and interesting-looking envelope for me in the morning's post from the New South Wales Government, and I opened it with an eagerness born of nearly two months's frustration.

In it, among other things, was a large map of Lord Howe Island, published in 1966. It was a good map with every feature marked, even to the various flag-staffs.

And there, in the middle of Prince William Henry Bay was the island that had been named after David Blackburn. It was not a very big island.Its area was 36 acres, two roods and a bit. But 36 acres is not to be sneezed at. At Itteringham there are about fifteen acres and a walk around our perimeter would be quite a distance. An acre if it be square, and if my mathematics are not at fault, would have each side measuring something over 69 yards. To walk round fifteen such squares all bunched together would mean traversing well over a thousand yards. But most acres are very far from square and by the time one has meandered, there would be little change out of a mile. On this basis a walk round the perimeter of this Pacific Island could mean walking the best part of two miles.

But there was one thing wrong. Grieviously wrong. It was not called Blackburn Island. It was called Rabbit Island. There could be no possible mistake about it. There it was, plainly marked— Rabbit Island. And the way leading to it through the coral reefs of the ocean that swept Lord Howe on its south western side was called Rabbit Island Passage. No wonder I had been unable to trace it in any modern reference book!

It is not difficult to imagine my feelings. It had taken me two months even to find the island. And now that it lay before me—this little stretch of earth that remained as a memorial to one man's efforts in the history of a nation—the name had gone. Even the local people who lived and worked on Lord Howe were oblivious of him.

Up in the north east corner of Lord Howe there is a geographical feature marked Jim's Point. I do not know who Jim was — but good luck to him! For some reason his name had been put down there — and it had remained. But Blackburn had been forgotten. Somehow, over the long years, as the waves broke against his island — that other tide of Time itself had crumbled away the last vestige of his memorial.

*   *   *

One of the extraordinary things about life is that it has a way of evening the score. Chance there may be. Luck and coincidence can be readily admitted. But there are also both harmony and order behind the universe, precision of timing and circumstance beyond our remotest conception.

For this reason, I did not believe on that January morning that these letters of David Blackburn had come to me by chance. I felt very strongly that they had fallen into the right hands at the right time. For one thing was certain to me then and there. He should have his island back again. If it took me one year, two years, ten years — his name should once more appear where it ought to appear — on the island that was named after him.

So, after breakfast, I wrote again to the Chairman of the Lord Howe Island Board asking him and his colleagues to consider giving the island back its original name.

"…Naturally (I wrote) it is not my wish to make a mountain out of a mole-hill or to try to make a continent out of a tiny island of some 36 acres, but I am very anxious indeed to try to get your co-operation in regard to seeing that something is done to preserve this little piece of your country's history…

…At this time, as I am sure you will agree, we are a little too close to the early history of Australia to appreciate fully exactly what these things may very well mean to those who come after us. It would be a great mistake for any part of history to be lost merely because a simple, but important, readjustment is not made at the right time.

May I please ask your Board to consider carefully the contents of this letter and to advise me by Air as soon as possible, to what extent you feel able to co-operate with the suggestions in it."

Incorporated in this letter, I also made an offer of a Memorial to David Blackburn in the following terms:

"I am willing to raise enough money here in England to provide a small Fund for the provision and maintenance of a seat to be installed on the island, the said seat to bear an inscription stating: 'This seat was given by the people of England in memory of David Blackburn, Master of H.M. Armed Tender Supply who sailed with the First Fleet to New South Wales in 1787 and after whom Blackburn Island was named on the 12th March, 1788'."

I air-mailed this letter and during the next few days thought much about it. I wished so much that I could have boarded a jet and been transported to Sydney to put my case, but this was out of the question. Even the petrol for my car makes too heavy demands upon our resources too often. There was nothing to do but wait again.

But supposing the people in Sydney were not interested! It seemed to me very unlikely that they would be. When one lives on a continent of three million square miles—what is some tiny island four hundred odd miles away in the Pacific? Was it likely that they would wish to disturb traditions that had endured for a hundred years or more? The chances were slim.

I realised that I had embarked upon a game of chess that might go on for a long time. But one thing was certain. No matter if it took ten years, this thing must be fought for until victory was achieved.

For fair is fair. Some men have stars named after them, or comets. And there, for a million years, their monuments shine in the darkness of outer space. Some have diseases named after them and for these, we must hope—as they themselves would assuredly hope—for a more temporary span of fame. Zachary Hicks, who was the first Lieutenant on board Captain Cook's ship, *The Endeavour,* had Point Hicks named after him. You can see it marked on any decent map of Australasia. He was the man who sighted it. And it bears his name. Others have buildings, streets, ponds, woods, recipes, trains or scientific laws named after them. And, for right or wrong, this thing is theirs. Nobody disputes it. Nobody envies it. But nobody forgets.

But here was a man who went out into the unknown at a time when the history of a great nation was being launched. He did his duty and he did it well.

"The very business like conduct" (wrote Governor Phillip to Mr

Stephens of the Admiralty) "of Mr David Blackburn as Master of the Supply and during the time he commanded that vessel while Lieut. Ball was sick on shore, make it a duty incumbent upon me to point him out as an officer deserving of their Lordships' notice."

The hazards he was obliged to face were very real. He was paid £5 per month. And by the time he was forty-two he was dead. He left £40 after his debts had been settled. Had there been the slightest opportunity of spending money in Australia he would scarcely have left a few shillings.

But he had a little green island named after him. He didn't even want the honour.

"I was on board whilst this ceremony was performing," (he wrote) "or it should have been called Knight Isle." Richard Knight was his special friend.

That little green island was his by right. His name should endure there as long as it remained above the waves. Not because he wanted it. Not because it would do him any good now. But because he was there when the *Supply* anchored in Prince William Henry Bay on the 12th March, 1788. He was there, right by this little island. His commander, Lieutenant Ball, named it after him — Blackburn Isle.

This was a fact of history. I had the proof before me in the original black and white of the man who wrote it.

Back at Sydney Cove, Mr Clark had the toothache. It is recorded. It is written down there in the diaries that Dr John Cobley edited so ably.

"Mr Clark developed a severe toothache..." Mr Clark "was very ill with the toothache all last night. Got up early and went to the hospital — and had it out by Mr Consident. Oh, my God what pain it was. It was so fast in, and the jaw-bone very fast to one of the prongs, the tooth would not come out without breaking the jaw-bone, which he did. I thought that half of my head would have come off..."

This is all history. Dr Cobley was right to see that everything was published in these wonderful diaries. The world wants to know what it was like to be in New South Wales as a member of the first colony. And in the coming centuries when men have emerged through the perils of their own ages to something approaching sanity — I do not doubt but that they will want to know even more what happened in the dawn of each nation's history.

So I wanted them to know, too, about Blackburn Island — a little green heap that is a monument to a man who deserves more from posterity than he ever got from his contemporaries.

*　　*　　*

As with all games of chess, one has to think ahead. So I used the waiting time to try to do just this.

The Mitchell Library in Sydney proved very helpful. For it was they who referred me to a book called *The Voyage of Governor Phillip to Botany Bay*, published in London by John Stockdale in 1791.

In this regard Fate was more than kind to me. One morning, I was talking to John Ferguson, one of the directors of Angus and Robertson in his London office and this book was mentioned. By some strange coincidence he had a copy of it in his safe — having acquired it only a little while before. And then and there he very kindly asked his secretary to produce for me a xerox copy of a chart of Lord Howe Island that appeared in it. It couldn't have been a much earlier one, for it was published in 1789. And there was the island plainly marked *Blackborn Island*. The mis-spelling was nothing. In those days almost every other word was spelled several different ways.

I then had a further stroke of luck. On a map published in Australia I came upon a reference to *The Geographical Names Act, 1966*. Naturally, anything that had to do with geographical names might be of interest, so I wrote to the New South Wales Government offices in London for a photostat of this Act. When it came, I found it rather long and forbidding. But I waded through it, and eventually came upon two interesting facts.

The first was that this Act — which was, of course, on the statute books of New South Wales — had to be administered by some rather important people. One, for instance, had to be the Surveyor General of New South Wales. And another — which pleased me immensely — had to be the Chief Librarian of New South Wales. And under Clause 5, Section H. the Act stated that one of the functions of the administering body should be:

"...to compile a dictionary of Geographical names, showing their...origin and history."

As soon as I read these words, I felt a sense of peace about the whole future of the project. I knew, then, that in the event of the Lord Howe Island Board being unwilling, for any reason, to pursue the matter — then the Geographical Names Act Board most certainly would. But so far, the Lord Howe Island Board had been courtesy itself. Perhaps among them there would be some who were historians and who would realise the importance of the adjustment that was needed.

*   *   *

On the 15th February, 1973 I received a letter from the Chairman, Mr J. B. Holliday, dated the 6th February. He wrote as follows:

I received your letter, dated 12th January, upon my return from holidays last week. Thank you for the interesting information outlined therein.

Your suggestion that the island now named Rabbit Island should revert to what you say is its original name, viz., Blackburn Island, will be placed before the Board at its March meeting. You will understand that some detailed research may be necessary and it could be some time after this before I am in a position to let you have definite information.

Your offer to provide and maintain a special seat on the island, with an appropriate plaque, is also very much appreciated and will be given due consideration by the Board.

Thank you again for the trouble taken in raising this matter. I shall write to you again as soon as I am in a position to do so.

Yours faithfully,
J. B. HOLLIDAY.
Chairman.

The next day, I sent by air the following letter.

J. B. Holliday, Esq.,   15th February, 1973.
Chairman,
The Lord Howe Island Board,
121, Macquarie Street,
Sydney, New South Wales.

Dear Sir,
Many thanks for your letter of the 6th February which I received this morning and from which I note that your Board

will give due consideration at your March meeting to the matter raised in mine of the 12th January last.

With a view to being helpful at this particular meeting, I venture to enclose herewith some further details concerning David Blackburn who has been the subject of my researches and I feel sure that these comments will assist you towards your decision.

Quite a number of people in this country are already very much interested in the project of providing a seat for the island and it is my hope to give talks to some of the schools in the region to interest the young people about this section of the early history of Australia. With the seat, if your Board is willing to accept our gift will be sent a book containing the names of all those who have made contributions towards it.

The seat will be made of English oak in the county of Norfolk by a craftsman and the suggested words will be carved in the wood itself. It will be sent ready for permanent assembly on Blackburn Island and all transport costs and assembly costs will be paid by our people out of the Fund provided.

We shall therefore look forward with the greatest possible interest to your eventual reply.

Yours sincerely,

With this letter was sent the following document.

The Case for giving Rabbit Island its original name of
Blackburn Island

1. In a letter written on the 12th July, 1788 by David Blackburn to Richard Knight, the following passage appears:

"At 4 o'clock in the afternoon we took possession of this island in the name of his Britannic Majesty and displayed the English colours and Mr Ball named the different parts of the island. The two mountains Mount Gower and Mount Lidgbird, the valley between them Erskine Valley, a large bay near the middle of the island Prince William Henry Bay, two other bays to the left of it Hunter Bay and Callam Bay and an island in the middle of Prince William Henry Bay, Blackburn Isle. Had I been present at this ceremony it should have been named Knight Island."

This passage is also included almost word for word in a letter from David Blackburn to his sister of the same date, the original of which is in my possession. The letter to Richard Knight is held by The Mitchell Library, reference AB 163, and together with another letter from David Blackburn to Richard Knight was published in full in the Royal Australian Historical Society Journal and Proceedings Volume 20, 1934, pages 318 to 334 also held by The Mitchell Library.

2. The Mitchell Library also holds a list of native names with English equivalents *compiled by David Blackburn,* reference AB 163, and copies of his letters to P. G. King, October 13th and October 25th, 1788, reference C187.

3. Blackburn commanded *The Golden Grove* on a voyage to Norfolk Island 25th September, 1788 and I hold the original directive in this regard signed by Phillip.

4. The Voyage of Governor Phillip to Botany Bay...compiled from authentic papers...to which are added the journals of Lieutenants Shortland, Watts, Ball and Captain Marshall... London, John Stockdale, 1791 (Mitchell Library reference Q991/P) contains a chart of Lord Howe Island discovered by Lieutenant Henry Lidgbird Ball in H.M. Armed Tender *Supply* on the 17th February, 1788, opposite page 180, in which the small island in Prince William Henry Bay is named *Blackborn Isle.* In the map published in 1909 showing permissive occupancies, New South Wales Government Printer, Mitchell Library reference M3 819.1/1909/1, the island is given as Blackborn or Goat Island. Then in the map of 1957, Mitchell Library reference M3 819.1/1957/1 third edition the island is called Rabbit Island and of course in 1966 it is also Rabbit Island.

In this regard may I most respectfully draw your attention to your own Geographical Names Act, section 5, clause H, and in particular to the last three words of that clause.

Just in case you happen not to have the Act with you at your meeting, clause 5 says "Subject to this Act, the powers and functions of the Board shall be" — (then it gives various sub-clauses and eventually come to clause H which says) — "to compile and maintain a dictionary of Geographical Names of the record of their form, spelling, meaning, pronunciation, *origin and history.*"

I hope it will not be thought by the Board any impertinence on my part to bring this matter to your attention. I only do so for your own convenience at this particular meeting and because I am sure there must be those among you who would agree that this function is an important aspect of your work.

5. You gentlemen will recall that after the *Sirius* had been wrecked on Norfolk Island, the *Supply* was the only naval vessel in your area. When she left finally for England, Collins wrote "The services of this little vessel had endeared her and her officers and people, to this colony. The regret which we felt at parting with them was, however, lessened by the knowledge that they were flying from a country of want to one of abundance where we all hoped that the services they had performed would be rewarded by the attention and promotion to which they naturally looked up, and had an indisputable claim."

Now the *Supply* was commanded on two occasions by David Blackburn and at a time when it was in a terrible state of repair. But in spite of his command, and although he was always in a high position of authority above deck; although he had Governor Phillip's own recommendation to their Lordships at the Admiralty —he received no such promotion. Like the ship itself, he went home very much the worse for wear, worn out by over four years' service. No doubt the ship had a refit. But Blackburn died in a consumption in Hasler hospital less than three years later.

6. David Blackburn was on board the *Supply* when it left for Batavia on one of the most urgent missions undertaken during the first settlement, that is to say when the *Supply* was sent to Batavia for urgent supplies. At that time all the members of the settlement were under severe rations and all the boats were employed fishing and the fish was brought to the public square and distributed among people. The *Sirius* had already been wrecked and it must be borne in mind that David Blackburn as Master of the *Supply* would have been its chief navigator. What would have happened to the first settlement if the *Supply* had also been wrecked can be left to the imagination! As it was this trip succeeded in bringing from Batavia a Dutch ship with new supplies and undoubtedly saved the people of the first settlement.

7. In a letter to his sister in my possession (hitherto unpublished) Blackburn writes "About six weeks after our arrival the Dutch ship arrived and we were ordered to Norfolk to bring the officers and seamen of the late *Sirius* to Port Jackson, in order to their

going to England in the Dutch ship. Mr Ball's health not permitting him to go to sea the command of the *Supply* was given me till his recovery and I sailed on the 23rd January, 1791 and performed the voyage in five weeks and brought the whole of the *Sirius*'s ship's company 91 persons. They are now preparing for England and will sail in a week."

You will notice, gentlemen, that there is nothing very flowery about this! No mention of difficulties, no mention of risks, no mention of the deplorable condition of the little *Supply*. Just a few swift lines conveying information that was to become part of your history.

8. As you will know, there were only two naval vessels in the first fleet. The others were transports and store-ships. On those two vessels, apart from Phillip himself, there were nine of the rank of Master and upwards. Blackburn ranked among these nine, and was subsequently given the command of the *Supply* on the two occasions already mentioned.

9. In his letter to Richard Knight dated 12th July, 1788 David Blackburn writes regarding Norfolk Island "...and it was the 3rd March before we were able to land which we then effected with the greatest difficulty but found it would be impossible to land the stores or women on account of the violent seas which broke on the shore. We therefore went in search of some other spot with little hopes of success and on the morning of the 6th I was sent in a boat to explore the south coast part of the island and found an eligible place for landing and the next day we landed all the colony there with their provisions, stores, etc.; to this place, Lieutenant King, the Superintendent and Commander of Norfolk, gave the name of Sydney Bay." Bearing in mind, gentlemen, that the *Sirius* was eventually wrecked on the coast of Norfolk Island, this effort of Blackburn's was not without considerable merit at that time.

I venture to send you these facts, gentlemen, for your convenience at this meeting and in order to save you unnecessary research and I think you will agree that there is a very strong case indeed for David Blackburn being remembered in Australian history. What you are being asked to do is not to change the name of some particular piece of your geography but to give back to this island its own original name so that it will remain there in the future as a small and well-deserved tribute to a man who played a real part in early Australian history.

My book, when it appears, will endeavour to give a picture of David Blackburn's contribution to the founding of the first settlement. He was a citizen of Norwich, Norfolk, and I shall be using fifteen hitherto unpublished letters written by him to his sister and others and also letters from his sister to New South Wales. I would naturally like to include in this book an account of your co-operation in this matter and to be able to say that, because of it, this small island has been given back its original name as a tribute to a man who deserved the thanks of the Australian people.

Yours sincerely,
Derek Neville.

I sealed this despatch with the distinct feeling that I had done all that could be done for the present. There was nothing to do now but to wait and see. Certainly I had the feeling that Mr J. B. Holliday, the Chairman of the Lord Howe Island Board, was on my side. One gets something from letters, apart from the actual typewritten content. And I had the impression that I was dealing with a man of integrity who would take whatever action he thought to be right.

I just wished, at that moment, that Australia was not quite so far away and that time could be speeded up.

Interlude

Again, I had to wait. This time, for nearly four months.

Through the good offices of the Postmaster on Lord Howe Island, I had established contact with a resident, Jean Brearley, who wrote me letters and sent me photographs of Rabbit Island. And in my mind I heard the Pacific breaking there. I saw the *Supply* at anchor, and the long-boat being pulled ashore for the first time, and the turtles curiously peering and the birds flying down to see. I saw the un-named mountains and the un-named bays. And the little island in the sun there, only a pin-prick in the ocean. But it grew bigger and bigger in my mind — not in size but in importance. Because this was his island, his memorial. It was the only thing he had left.

CHAPTER TWELVE

The Loss of The *Guardian*

THE first fleet went out with a cargo of ordinary human beings drawn from all parts of England. Marines, officers, convicts—most of them leaving behind those who would remember them as long as they lived. In most cases, that parting prior to the 13th May, 1787 was a final parting. Very few of those who left England on that date were ever seen again by those they left behind, no matter how close or dear they may have been.

David Blackburn's sister Margaret was one such person. She appears to have been deeply attached to her brother, but in a most possessive way. As we have already seen, she missed the opportunity of a last meeting with him at Portsmouth. She could so easily have made the journey there at his expense, cold or no cold. But she declined and he sailed away without any last glimpse of her. She never saw him again and one suspects that her own sense of guilt was very largely responsible for the emotional breakdown she suffered after she learnt of his death in 1795.

Be that as may, two long letters that she wrote to him from Norwich have survived and these are included in full in the Appendix.

In the first, there is an amusing description of a balloon ascent—one of several made in Norwich around that time, when various intrepid adventurers vied with each other in such matters.

"Do not wonder," wrote Horace Walpole to Sir H. Mann on the 2nd December, 1783. "Do not wonder that we do not entirely attend to things of earth; fashion has ascended to a higher element. All our views are directed to the air. Balloons occupy senators, philosophers, ladies, everybody".

With regard to the second surviving letter from Margaret Blackburn, dated 9th September, 1789 (see Appendix) there are some interesting sidelights. It was put in the care of Captain Riou of the *Guardian*, together with three parcels which had been sent to Portsmouth in the spring of 1788. She wrote:

"I hope the good Captain and ship to whom the conveyance of this and three packets of letters, newspapers, etc., of different dates from me are committed, will be favoured by the elements and every possible advantage that can render their passage quick, safe and pleasant."

Her hope was not to be fulfilled, however, for the *Guardian* was wrecked off the Cape of Good Hope on the 23rd December, 1789.

This misfortune was one of the greatest tragedies in the early years of the New South Wales Settlement, and was to mean great hardship for those who had been waiting so long for relief from England.

A graphic description is given by Tench on the 3rd June when the *Lady Juliana* at last reached Sydney Cove:

"I was sitting in my hut, musing on our fate, when a continued clamour in the street drew my attention. I opened my door, and saw several women with children in their arms running to and fro with distracted looks, congratulating each other, and kissing their infants with the most passionate and extravagant marks of fondness. I needed no more; but instantly started out, and ran to a hill, where by the assistance of a pocket-glass, my hopes were realised.

My next door neighbour, a brother officer, was with me; but we could not speak; we wrung each other by the hand, with eyes and hearts over-flowing.

As we proceeded, the object of our hopes soon appeared: — a large ship, with English colours flying, working in, between the heads which formed the entrance of the harbour. The tumultuous state of our minds represented her in danger; and we were in agony. Soon after, the Governor, having ascertained what she was, left us, and stepped into a fishing boat to return to Sydney. We pushed through wind and rain, the anxiety of our sensations every moment re-doubling. At last we read the word London on her stern. 'Pull away, my lads! She is from old England! A few strokes more, and we shall be aboard! Hurrah for a belly-ful, and news from our friends!' — such were our exhortations to the boat's crew. A few minutes completed our wishes, and we found ourselves on board the Lady Juliana transport with 225 of our countrywomen whom crime or misfortune had condemned to exile. We learned that they had been almost eleven months on their passage, having left Plymouth, into which port they had been put in July, 1789.

Captain John Hunter succeeded Captain Phillip as Governor of New South Wales.
A drawing by R. Dighton engraved by D. Orme and published in September 1972.

Mansell Collection

(xi)   Australia's first Flagship, H.M.S. *Sirius* commanded by Captain John Hunter.

Australian News and Information Bure

(xii) A silhouette appears to be the only surviving illustration of David Blackburn.

ii) A Norfolk Island 3 cent stamp issue records Blackburn's ship, H.M.S. *Supply.*
P. A. Vicary, Cromer

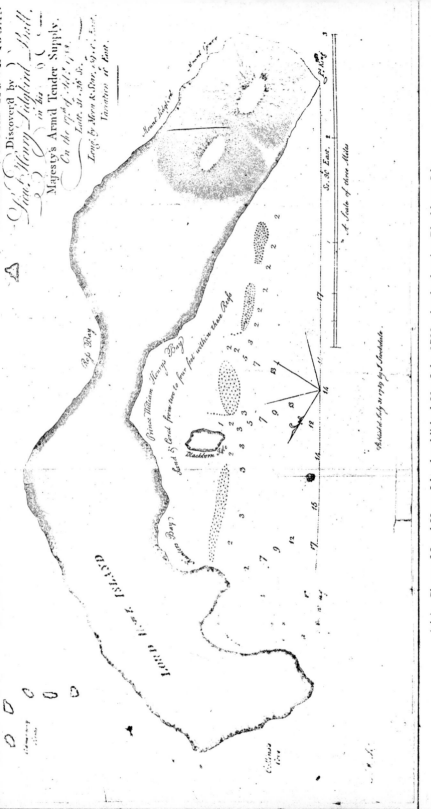

(xiv)   Chart of Lord Howe Island published 31st July, 1789, clearly showing Blackburn Isle.

(xv)   Blackburn Isle lying in the large bay formed by Lord Howe Island.

(xvi)   The seat, made of Norfolk oak by Joe Dawes who is in the picture, and transported to Flagstaff Hill on Lord Howe Island and sited to look over Blackburn Isle. It was made of wood from and by a craftsman living in Blackburn's county of birth, and was given by the people of England in memory of David Blackburn.

Eastern Counties Newspapers, Norwich

(vii) A convict being flogged at Botany Bay; by R. Caton Woodville. *Mansell Collection*

This is no otherwise curious than as a specimen of the first efforts / of Engraving in Van Diemens land —

HOBART TOWN CHAIN GANG.

Sent home from Van Diem / 1031

(xviii)   Hobart Town Chain Gang. "This is no otherwise curious than as a specimen of th
first efforts at engraving in VanDiemansland" comment of recipient in 1831.

Mansell Collectio

(xix)   In 1973 a fifteen million Australian Dollar restoration scheme was started in the Ea
Rocks area of Sydney, the cradle of the Australian nation. Picture shows Cadma
Cottage, oldest surviving house being restored.

Australian Information Service Photograph by John Tann

We continued to ask a thousand questions on a breath. Stimulated by curiousity, they enquired in turn; but the right of being first answered, we thought, lay on our side. 'Letters! Letters!' was the cry. They were produced, and torn open in trembling agitation. News burst upon us like meredian splendour or a blind man. We were over-whelmed with it; public, private, general and particular."

No doubt there were many who were overjoyed at receiving news from home that day in Port Sydney. But it must be left to our imagination to consider the dreadful tragedy that must have struck so many on the mainland of New South Wales. For it soon emerged that the *Guardian* with all its provisions and stocks had come to grief and one does not doubt that many letters and packages intended for the convicts, settlers, and officers, were lost for ever.

Indeed, as I look at this letter before me written so long ago by Margaret Blackburn, I find myself wondering how it came to be in England. Did it ever reach David Blackburn? Was it eventually found among his effects after his death and returned to his sister? Or was it never, in fact, delivered, but returned to its sender? Fortunately we know the answers. Both letters — the one from his sister and the one from Richard Knight reached Blackburn safely. Mention is, in fact, made of the latter in the official record. Blackburn was away in the *Batavia* at the time of the *Lady Juliana*'s arrival at Sydney Cove but on his return to Port Jackson on the 19th October there was an entry in the records "David Blackburn took delivery of a letter from Mr Richard Knight." As to the letter from Margaret Blackburn — this is mentioned in his own letter dated 17th March, 1791. Certain other packages probably never reached him.

But to return to the *Guardian,* this ship had been fitted out most admirably and Collins, writing in detail of the effects on the Colony of the loss of the *Guardian,* says:

"His Majesty's ship Guardian, of 44 guns, commanded by Lieutenant Edward Riou, sailed from England, having on board, with what was in the Lady Juliana, two years' provisions, mainly viz. 295,344 pounds of flour, 149,856 pounds of beef and 303,632 pounds of pork, for the settlement; a supply of clothing for the marines serving on shore, and for those belonging to the Sirius and Supply; together with a large quantity of sails and cordage for those ships and for the uses of the Colony; sixteen chests of medicines; fifteen casks of wine; a quantity of blankets and bedding for the hospital; and a large supply of unmade clothing for the convicts; with an ample assortment of tools and implements of agriculture."

When the *Guardian* struck an island of ice, the Captain was compelled to throw overboard the greatest part of her valuable cargo both public and private. The stock was all killed, (seven horses, sixteen cows, two bulls, a number of sheep, goats and two deer).

So instead of the *Guardian* arriving with supplies sufficient for two years, the *Lady Juliana* arrived carrying a cargo of 225 female convicts instead of provisions. Collins wrote of the 6th June, 1790:

"The supply of provisions on board however so inconsiderable as to permit an addition of one pound and a half of flour being made to the weekly ration. Had the Guardian arrived, perhaps we should never again have been in want."

Incidentally the *Lady Juliana* had taken some ten or eleven months to make the journey from England to Australia.

In the book *Australia, Her Story* by Kylie Tennant, it is stated,

"The ship, the Juliana, carried no food. She brought over 200 prostitutes, and the news that the supply ship had been wrecked off the Cape of Good Hope. Over 200 useless mouths to eat their provisions! The voyage had lasted eleven months and the women were in bad shape."

This information is rather contradicted by a writer quoted in *Sydney Cove* who says:

"The Lady Juliana had on board 225 female convicts, with two years' provisions for them only; they were remarkably healthy throughout the voyage, most likely from the judicious plan of affording them tea, sugar, and soap, with frequent refreshments by the way."

If, as one supposes, these female convicts had been sent out as a wise relief for the men isolated in the new settlement, it is more than likely that they would have received many benefits on the voyage out — probably in return for favours granted!

*   *   *

One can imagine Margaret Blackburn sitting in her house in Magdalen Street, Norwich, writing to her brother in September,

1789. Little did she know that the vessel on which it was carried was to be involved in disaster — bringing about a severe hardship for all those who had gone out in the First Fleet including her brother.

I have gazed at this letter for long and long, the broken red seal still on it, the handwriting addressed to Blackburn at Botany Bay c/o Captain Riou — and I have wondered what happened to it before it found the calmer waters of 1974.

One thing is certain. It was eventually received by David Blackburn in Port Sydney on the 19th October, 1790, as already stated, after his return from Batavia (see his own letter dated 17th March, 1791) together with Richard Knight's letter which most probably travelled in the *Lady Juliana*.

It had taken one year and forty days to reach him. It had suffered shipwreck and near disaster. But it got there in the end!

Not only did it get there — but, magically enough, it got back to England again and was presumably found among Blackburn's possessions after his death. So that I have it here in front of me now, a faded letter impregnated with history.

Margaret Blackburn went to pieces after her brother's death in 1795. There are a number of letters existing in which her friends and relatives do their best to console her and to make her see the uselessness of her prolonged and morbid grief.

I wish she could have seen this book. Perhaps the sight of her own letters achieving their own modicum of fame would have succeeded where her friends and relatives failed!

But we have to work out our own salvation in our own time, doing our best, as David Blackburn himself did, from day to day and letting eternity adjust matters as it surely will.

*   *   *

Perhaps one of the most curious things about history is in regard to this matter of adjustment. The true importance of any given event can seldom be seen when we are close to it. A poet or writer may be ignored or even scorned in his own day — but history will adjust the matter in its own time. The inventor, close to his immediate problems, can rarely look ahead to the crowning glory of his achievements — no matter how unbounded his enthusiasms! Somewhere, no doubt, in that twilight, before the dawn of history, some unknown person, conceived the first wheel. But one doubts whether he saw its full and ultimate potential!

I have searched in the early Norfolk newspapers for any mention of the historic First Fleet sailing on the 13th May, 1787 — but in vain. That expedition did not make the headlines until much later, until men had sweated and died and written their little accounts of immediate events, until the first houses in Sydney had been erected, until the settlement grew into a town, and began to sprawl upon the barren land around it, in fact, until the whole mighty vista of modern Australia had begun to open up.

For it is true to say that only in comparatively recent years have Australians become really interested in what went on in the old days before, when the difference between starvation and salvation was a ship.

They used to think they sprang from convicts. Now it is abundantly plain that the real convicts were those who sent out those transports of oppressed humanity, unable to conform to laws which kept them below the starvation line. Over the years, they were able to free themselves, to stretch out their arms towards their dreams that had never really died. Perhaps it took a generation or two. No doubt there were tragedies beyond telling. But they had their dreams, those little people in the time before. And the years could not bury them.

For they were not content with mere dreams.

> "Dreams is alright, honey-child.
> I ain't got nuth'n against dreams
> But they ain't never no good
> By theirselves.
> They don't get no place.
> They just melts away
> Like sump'n that ain't never been
> Nowhere.
> A stationary dream ain't nuthin
> More'n an empty mind.
> But you get a dream movin' honey-flower.
> An' it'll slide down the rainbow
> Like butter on a hot knife.
>
> Take this here wheel.
> This was a dream once.

84

Somebody sat down one day
Tired as a wore-out shoe
Blistered and beat
On account of carryin' more things
Than he could remember,
Till he was all done up
Like an ol' lettuce leaf.
So he sits there in the hot sun
One day before history started,
An' this dream come tumblin' down
Into his mind
Big as a brontasaurus.

So he got started.
He chopped an' he chiselled
He wopped an' he shaped
Till his dream was round
Like he'd seen it in the first place.
But then, honey-flower,
He din't just sit there
Pattin' himself on the back
Waitin' fer sump'n to happen
No Sir!
He pushed an' he shoved
Till he got his dream movin'
An that wheel, honey-child,
It ain't never really stopped since."

And the Australian people certainly pushed until they got their
dream moving. That is why they have my ungrudging admiration —
and I hope they will accept these remarks from a mere 'Pommy' as a
tribute to their strength, virility and forthrightness which have
sprung out of their past.

Back in England, at that time, Parson Woodforde was writing his
diaries. A glance or two at them would not be out of place.

1780. September 22nd. I stayed and drank a dish of coffee with
the Squire and one Mr Martineau of Norwich, a Doctor and Man
Midwife.

John Beresford the Editor of Parson Woodforde's Diaries (1924)
says in a footnote: "Doubtless an ancestor — possibly grandfather,
certainly a kinsman of the famous 19th Century Martineaus Harriet
and her brother James." There is not much doubt, however, that

this was Philip Meadows Martineau who was then assistant surgeon at the Norfolk and Norwich Hospital.

1785. April 12. Mr Peachman called here about 7 o'clock and paid me for 4 acres of turnips at 30s. per acre.

April 18. Saw the first swallow this season this morning.

April 22. After breakfast Nancy went with me in Lenewade Chaise to Aylsham it being the Archdeacon's Generals there today — Nancy was obliged to dine by herself at our Inn, the 3 Black Boys.

June 1st. About 3 o'clock this afternoon a violent tempest arose at Norwich in the North East, very loud thunder with strong white lightening with heavy rain — which lasted about an hour — immediately after which Mr Decker's Balloon with Decker himself in a boat annexed to it, ascended from Quantrells Gardens and very majestically.

1786. April 9th. To a poor deaf Man from Mattishall gave 1 penny.

July 13th. We had for dinner some Pyke and Fryed Soals, a nice piece of boiled beef, Ham and a couple of fowls, peas and beans, a Green Goose roasted, Gooseberry pies, Currant Tarts, The Charter, hung beef scraped etc. For supper Fryed Soals, a couple of chickens roasted, cold ham, etc. etc. Artichokes, Tarts, etc. Fruit after dinner and supper — strawberries, cherries, Almonds, Raisins, etc. etc.

June 28. Billy Bidewell came to me this morning to desire me to lend him a few guineas — but I could not.

December 12. Poor Tom Twaites of Honingham who was beat by the Poachers at Mr Townshends the other day is lately dead of the wounds he then received from them.

1788. January 13. Mr Custance not at church, he being detained on Justice business, having had a felon by name Wakefield of Boston brought to him this afternoon on very great suspicion of his being guilty of the Murder of one Thos. Twaites of Honingham, when a great many poachers were at Mr Townshends about 3 years ago.

All the above from The Diary of a Country Parson,
The Reverend James Woodforde.

86

During all the time between the sailing of the First Fleet on 13th May, 1787 and its arrival at Botany Bay on the 18th January, 1788, there is no mention in Parson Woodforde's diaries of the event, as far as I can discover. In his remote country parsonage, he was far removed from such events, being more concerned with what he ate, while others starved. Though history was in the making, this voyage to a new land was hardly in the realm of his experience.

CHAPTER THIRTEEN

Notes Concerning Some Passengers

Among the Blackburn letters I came across the following directive from Governor Phillip dated 19th March, 1791:

CIVIL

Mr Thomas Jamieson

SETTLERS

Owen Cavanagh
James Proctor
James Painter
William Hambly
Robert Watson
William Mitchell
Peter Ibbs
John Drummond
Samuel King
Charles Heritage

NEW SOUTH WALES CORP.

William Hill — Capt.
Edward Abbott — Lieut.

Jn. Thos. Prentice	Ens.
Jas Breckenrig	Serg.
Jn. Gardner	Corp.
John Dell	Drummer
John Abrahams	Private
Joseph Baylis	,,
Thomas Boulton	,,
James Capey	,,
Theoph. Feuterell	,,
John Haycock	,,
Will. Hook	,,
Edw. Hemmings	,,
Thomas Lloyd	,,
Joseph Lunn	,,
James Morris	,,
Robert Middleton	,,
John Miller	,,
Charles McCarty	,,
Samuel Marsden	,,
Lachlan Ross	,,

By His Excellency, Arthur Phillip, Esq., Captain General and Governor in Chief, in and over His Majesty's Territory of New South Wales and its Dependencies, etc. etc.

Whereas Lieutenant Henry Lidgbird Ball is from sickness unable to proceed to sea with H.M. Armed Tender Supply, of which you are Master, and I think fit that you should command her during his absence, or until you receive Orders.

You are hereby required and directed to take upon you the charge and command of the said Armed Tender accordingly. And, having received on board the Stores which the Commissary has been directed to send for the use of the settlers on Norfolk Island and the officers, soldiers and others named in the Margin, you are immediately to proceed to Norfolk Island; where you will land the said Peoples, Stores etc. and having received on board such Persons as the Commanding Officer on the Island may send, with as large a Quantity of Deals, Oars or other Articles for the Use of this Settlement as you can conveniently stow, you are to return to this Port, without further Loss of Time.

Zach. Sherrard   ,,
Joseph White   ,,

Male Convicts
Moses Tucker
Jonathan Griffiths
William Knight
Jeremiah Porter   For which this shall be your Order

                                  Government House, Sydney
                                  this 19th March, 1791
                                  (sgd.) A. Phillip.

To Mr David Blackburn
   Hereby appointed to command
   His Majesty's Armed Tender
      SUPPLY
   By Command of His Excellency
   (sgd.) David Collins
         Secretary.

Seeing the names in the margin, and being consumed with curiosity as to what had happened to the various people mentioned, I referred to the official record, and the following bits of information emerged:

Of the settlers, I could find no trace of any but two. There was a James Proctor buried on the 12th March 1792 at Parramatta, but he was a convict and his name may have been coincidental.

However, William Hambly, whose name is among the settlers, would seem to be a carpenter's mate on H.M.S. *Sirius.* On the 21st March, 1791 he gave evidence before Magistrates at the trial of a prisoner suspected of having stolen some carpenter's tools. The prisoner was discharged. Again on Thursday the 8th September, he returned from Norfolk Island with another settler named William Phillimore in order to be a witness at the trial of Thomas Jones. The verdict of the court was "acquitted, for want of evidence". This trial took place a week after their return to New South Wales on Thursday the 15th September and Collins, who signed the papers, made some interesting comments about the trial, as follows:

"Great inconvenience was experienced from having to send prisoners from the island with all the necessary witnesses. In the case just mentioned the prosecutor was a settler, who being obliged to leave his farm for the time, the business of which was necessarily suspended until he could return was ruined; and one of the witnesses was nearly in the same situation. But, as the courts in New South Wales would always be the superior courts, it was not easy to discover a remedy for these inconveniences."

The other settler of whom we find some trace is William Mitchell, and in his regard we find a human story, condensed into a very few lines. The first entry is dated Sunday 26th October, 1788:

"The twin sons of William Mitchell, a marine, and of Jane Fitzgerald, a convict, were christened William and James Mitchell."

Then, on Thursday the 15th January, 1789 we find this brief entry:

"James Mitchell Fitzgerald, a convict's child, was buried."

I must admit to feeling very moved when I came across these two brief entries. What depths of experience must lie behind them! The young marine, falling in love with a convict — of whom perhaps he had charge. The eventual birth of twins to the woman, Jane Fitzgerald; the hopes and fears that must have passed between them as he went about his duties and as she was confined to her sorry state; the dreams they had together of one day starting a new life in a new land. And then, one of the children buried before it was three months old.

There is strong reason to believe that William Mitchell's children were the first twins to be born of white parents in the continent of Australia!

But, to me at least, the real beauty and humanity of this episode from a half-buried past lies in the name given to the child at its burial. James Mitchell Fitzgerald. It could so easily have been called merely James Fitzgerald — or just James Mitchell. These two lovers — for I have no doubt at all but that it was real love — could not be legally married in their separate states, one a marine and the other a convict. But in that gesture, laid like a flower upon the grave, they united their names and by some quirk of fate have achieved a kind of immortality in the early history of Australia.

Let us hope that William Mitchell was eventually able to marry Jane Fitzgerald after she had served her sentence, that the remaining child survived and that somewhere in Australia today their descendants thrive.

The same William Mitchell incidentally, crops up once more on the 17th July, 1791 when he gives evidence in the defence of two soldiers named Norris and Roberts, against whom a very serious charge of theft had been made. Both men were found not guilty.

Only one of the four convicts mentioned in the margin of the above letter of whom there is certain mention is Moses Tucker. On the 1st November 1788, he was charged with stealing five boards from the Lieutenant Governor's yard, found guilty, and was sentenced to two hundred lashes. However, he only received part of his punishment, being forgiven the rest.

Again, on the 1st August, 1790, when the *Surprise* sailed for Norfolk Island, Scott wrote:

"One Tucker, a convict carpenter, is supposed to have made his escape in the above-mentioned ship Surprise."

It is possible that Jonathan Griffiths was, in fact, John Griffiths, a convict who was buried at Rosehill, on Tuesday, 31st May, 1791

Nothing is known of William Knight but, again, Jeremiah Porter could well be a convict mentioned as Zechy Porter who was buried at Parramatta on Saturday 4th February, 1792.

Among those mentioned under the heading of "New South Wales Corp", nothing is known of sixteen of the names. Both John Dell and Charles McCarty however, crop up on the 26th August, 1790 in Scott's diary when he reports that Private James McManus was confined,

"...for Stealing a Chest containing several Articles, The property of Charles McCarty of the New South Wales Corps. The same day McManus Informed the Commanding Officer that 'he Received the Articles that was found on him from Jn. Dell, a Drummer of the South Wales Corps.' Upon this Information the Drummer was Confined."

James Morris could possibly be a man named Morris mentioned only in regard to a possible attempt at escape on the 20th September, 1790 and Lachlan Ross might possibly be a man referred to as "Mr Ross, the Gunner" in an entry made by Collins on the 19th October 1790. This is more than likely and, in the event, he was buried at Batavia some time after the 6th July of that year.

William Hook might possibly be a convict of that name who was buried at Parramatta on the 11th February, 1792.

Jn. Thos. Prentice was included in a return of the New South Wales Corps. enclosed with Philip's letter to Grenville of the 14th

July, 1790 and in the same return it was noted that three privates had died since October 22nd 1789, and that one drummer and six privates had deserted. This may very well account for my inability to find out anything further about some of these names. Ensign Prentice, however, is discovered marching against the natives on Wednesday 22nd December 1790, under Tench, and on the 7th March 1791, his name is mentioned as an officer designated for Norfolk Island, where surely enough, he is sent on board the Tender *Supply* on the 21st March, and his presence is confirmed there on Saturday 22nd October, 1791.

Lieutenant Edward Abbott is also mentioned in a return of the New South Wales Corps. on the 24th July, 1790.

According to John Harris, Lieutenant Abbott was also in the small party of men who went to Broken Bay where there was a serious incident with the natives, on Tuesday 7th September, 1790. During this incident, Governor Arthur Phillip was wounded by a spear thrown at him. It struck him a little below the shoulder and pierced right through and came out four or five inches the opposite side. He appears to have been extremely fortunate in not having lost his life. Extraordinary as it may seem, the party had with them only four muskets and when the need arose to fire them only one of them could be made to work.

Abbott next appears in an entry of the 2nd October, 1790 when he is requested to attend a court to be held on the 4th October. He again appears with Ensign Prentice on the 22nd December in an expedition against the natives under Tench. In 1791 he is included with Mr Prentice as one of the three officers designated for Norfolk Island (7th March). On the 21st March, he sails in the *Supply* again in the company of Ensign Prentice and Captain Hill, and the last we hear of him is on the 22nd October, 1791 in a memo from Governor Phillip to Lieutenant King in which he says "Lieutenant Abbott and Ensign Prentice are to remain at Norfolk Island under the Command of Captain Patterson."

The final member of the New South Wales Corps. whose activities we are able to follow is Captain William Hill.

On 24th July, 1790 he is mentioned in a return of the New South Wales Corps. by Captain Nicholas Nepean as a joint captain with himself.

On Saturday 28th August, Scott enters in his diary dated wrongly as:

"Saturday 29th August, Captains Tench and Hill...returned after a week's excursion to the Northward of Rose Hill. Found a very bad country a distance from Prospect Hill. Sandy ground covered with brush wood. They fell in with an arm of Hawksburys river, traced it two days."

On Tuesday, 14th December, 1790, Captain Hill sets off with an expedition under Tench against the natives. Their instructions are to capture six natives if possible, or otherwise to shoot six natives. If six were captured, it was intended to hang two of them and to send the rest to Norfolk Island for a certain period. This action was considered necessary in view of the fact that several people had been attacked by natives. In fact Governor Phillip declared that since their arrival in the country seventeen people had either been killed or wounded by the natives. The expedition set off but was completely unsuccessful. They returned without having wounded or hurt a native, or made a prisoner. Whenever the party was seen by the natives they fled with incredible swiftness. Scott wrote that the "detachment returned but could not put their orders in execution."

On Monday 26th July, Captain Hill wrote to Mr Wathen. His letter is of very great interest because it gives a vivid picture of the unhappy conditions endured by convicts in certain of the transports of that time (1790). His letter was a long one and I do not propose to quote the whole of it but the following extracts will suffice.

"The bark I was on board of was, indeed, unfit, from her make and size, to be sent so great a distance; if it blew but the most trifling gales she was lost in the waters, of which she shipped so much that, from the Cape, the unhappy wretches, the convicts, were considerably above their waists in water, and the men of my company, whose berths were not so far forward, were nearly up to the middles. In this situation they were obliged, for the safety of the ship, to be pinned down; but when the gales abated no means were used to purify the air by fumigations, no vinegar was applied to rectify the nauseous steams issuing from their miserable dungeons. Humanity shudders to think that of nine hundred male convicts embarked in this fleet, three hundred and seventy are already dead and four hundred and fifty are landed sick and so emaciated and helpless that very few, if any of them, can be saved by care or medicine, so that the sooner it pleases God to remove them the better it will be for this colony, which is not a situation to bear any burthen, as I imagine the medicine chest to be nearly exhausted and provisions are a scarce article. The irons used upon these unhappy wretches were barborous. The contractors had been in the Guinea trade and had put on board the same shackles used by them in that trade, which are made with a short bolt, instead of chains that dropped between the legs and fastened with a bandage above the waist, like those at the different jails; these bolts were not more than three-quarters of a foot in length, so that they could not extend either leg from the other more than an inch or two at most; thus fettered, it was impossible for them to move but at the risk of both legs being broken. Inactivity at sea is a sure bane as it invites the scurvy equal to, if not more than, salt provisions; to this they were consigned, as well as a miserable pittance of provisions, although the allowance by Government is ample; even when attacked by disease their situations were not altered, neither had they any comforts administered. The slave trade is merciful compared with what I have seen in this fleet; in that it is in the interests of the masters to preserve the healths and lives of their captives, they having a joint benefit with the owners; in this, the more they can withhold from the unhappy wretches the more provisions they have to dispose of at a foreign market, and the earlier in the voyage they die the longer they can draw the deceased's allowance to themselves; for I fear few of them are honest enough to make a just return of the dates of their deaths to their employers."

On Saturday, the 22nd October, Governor Phillip wrote to Lieutenant King an instruction in which he mentions Captain Hill, saying:

"Captain Hill that part of his company now under his command is relieved by Captain Patterson and his company in the duty of that settlement (Norfolk Island) will embark in the Queen transport which will follow in a few days."

On Tuesday the 13th December 1791, we find a most interesting mention of Captain Hill in a letter that a Mr Johnson wrote to J. Stonard. In this he says:

"There have been and are great differences among our officers here. Yesterday a dual was fought between Major Ross and a Captain Hill—I wish that after the marines are gone home we may be more peaceable, but I fear whether dissensions will not prevail as bad as ever. Fortunately neither party was wounded yesterday and after two fires on each side the seconds interfered and settled the difference."

Monday, 21st March:

"Captain Hill of the New South Wales Corps. with Lieutenant Abbott and Ensign Prentice with one sergeant, one corporal, one drummer and eighteen privates embarked on board H.M. Armed Armed Tender Supply for the relief of the same number of marines at Norfolk Island."

Tuesday, 22nd March, Tench wrote:

"The indefatiguable Supply again sailed for Norfolk Island carrying thither Captain Hill under a detachment of New South Wales Corps. A little native boy named Bon-del, who had long particularly attached himself to Captain Hill, accompanied him, at his own earnest request. His father had been killed in battle and his mother had been bitten in two by a shark; so that he was an orphan dependant upon the humanity of his tribe for protection."

This is all the information I can discover about any of the names of the people who travelled with David Blackburn on the *Supply* to Norfolk Island on the 19th March, 1791.

CHAPTER FOURTEEN

A Gallant Ship

FROM the 17th day of January, 1791 and throughout that spring until, at least, the 30th May, David Blackburn was in command of the *Supply*.

Among the original documents that have survived, there are two directives signed by Phillip as follows:

By his Excellency Arthur Phillips, Esq., Captain General and Governor in Chief in and over H.M. Majesty's territory of New South Wales and its Dependencies, whereas Lieutenant Henry Lidgbird Ball is from sickness unable to proceed to sea with His Majesty's Armed Tender Supply of which you are Master and I think fit that you should command her during his absence as until you shall receive further orders you are hereby required and directed to take upon you the charge and command of the said Armed Tender accordingly and proceed without loss of time to Norfolk Island where having landed the stores and provisions which have been put on board by H.M. Commissiary for that purpose as well as (?) and other provisions as you can conveniently spare for the use of that settlement you are to receive on board the officers, seamen, mariners, late belonging to H.M. ship Sirius with whom you are to return to this port for which this shall be your order.

> Government House, Sydney,
> The 17th day of January, 1791
> (sgd.) A. Phillip

To Mr David Blackburn, hereby appointed to command H.M. Armed Tender Supply by His Excellency's commands

> David Collins, Secretary.

And again:

By His Excellency Arthur Phillips, Esq., Captain General and Governor in Chief in and over His Majesty's territory of New South Wales and its Dependencies

Whereas Lieutenant Henry Lidgbird Ball is from sickness unable to proceed to sea with H.M. Armed Tender Supply of which you are Master and I think fit that you should command her during his absence or until you shall receive further orders, you are hereby required and directed to take upon you the charge of command of the said Armed Tender accordingly and having received on board the stores which the Commissiary has been directed to send you for the use of the settlers on Norfolk Island of the officers, soldiers and others named in the margin you are immediately to proceed to Norfolk Island where you will land the said peoples, stores, etc. and having received on board such persons as the Commanding Officer on the Island may send with as large a quantity of deals oars and other articles for the use of their Settlement as you can conveniently stow you are to return to this port without further loss of time for which this shall be your order

Government House, Sydney,
this 19th March, 1791
(sgd.) A. Phillip.

To Mr David Blackburn, hereby appointed to command H.M. Armed Tender Supply by command of His Excellency, David Collins,

Secretary.

The following is quoted from *Early Explorers in Australia*, (Lee):

"The Supply was a wonderful little ship and it has been said that she was ever the harbinger of glad welcome tidings. Described as a very firm strong little brig, she mounted eight guns and was purchased by the Admiralty to take the place of the Grantham when that ship was proved unseaworthy. While the complement of the Sirius numbered 160 men that of the Supply was but 55. Under Lieutenant Ball, as tender to the frigate, she helped to escort the transports and store-ships to New South Wales and seems to have been especially favoured by Captain Phillip. When eighty leagues eastward of the Cape of Good Hope, he went on board the Supply, in order to hurry on in advance and choose a place for the reception of his fleet. To her, therefore, fell the honour of being the first ship to follow the Endeavour along the east coast. It has been told how she entered the harbour of Port Jackson a day before the other vessels in 1788. While stationed there she had a very useful career and made many voyages to Norfolk Island. She sailed from Sydney with the Sirius in March 1790. In the following month Captain Phillip despatched the brig on an important mission to Batavia. A little later she too was ordered home for re-fitting.

The Supply returned to England by way of Cape Horn, possibly in the track which the sailors had previously taken for on December 27th, 1791 she also reached the high latitude of 57° 32'S. On April 20th 1792, she sighted the Lizard."

This brief tribute to the *Supply* could well do with some amplification.

Those of us who have watched, on television screens, various astronauts on the barren surface of the moon must have realised, without any prodigious effort, what the Command Module meant to them. It was not only their link with home—it *was* their home. Yet those men, all of them, were never truly alone. They could speak with Houston by day or by night. They were in the hands of sophisticated computers designed to control their welfare. Without detracting one jot from their own bravery and skill—it can be truthfully said that the risks they ran were, in the event, less than the risk that fell to the lot of those who went out with the First Fleet.

To these people a ship, any ship, spelt Hope itself. And of all the ships known to that first small community, it was the indomitable little Brig—the *Supply*—that meant most to them during four lonely years, terrifying years of desolation, famine, doubt and fear. Time and time again, when things were going wrong—it was the *Supply* that sailed to the rescue. Notably, it was this little ship, with David Blackburn aboard, that rescued the whole settlement from an untimely end when she sailed for Batavia for fresh supplies, after the wreck of the *Sirius*. Had disaster overtaken her then—as well it might—then disaster would have followed for those who were already in desperate straits.

This little ship, this brave little ship, was buoyant with the hopes of all who knew her. By all the laws of logic, she ought to have been unable to keep afloat. But she voyaged on as though her timbers were impregnated with the determination to see things through. She must, herself, have been a symbol of courage to those whose own courage never wavered.

We have only to look at her closely during the last year of her association with the settlement to see the stuff she was made of!

At the end of May, 1791, when Blackburn returned with her to Sydney, Governor Phillip learned with concern that she required extensive repairs.

Really this should not have been surprising news to him. As will be seen from the above, she had been ordered home for refitting, after her return from Batavia. This would have been in October, 1790 — and on that voyage alone she had been absent from the settlement for over six months. But the *Sirius* had been wrecked during the previous February and this gallant little *Supply* was too much in demand to be spared.

Yet we find that on the 11th March, 1791, Robinson Reid, the carpenter of the *Supply*, had made a detailed report as to the condition of the ship — a report which had been marked "Approved" and signed by Lieutenant Ball.

"The main deck decayed, and to be made new fore and aft.
The head of the main mast decayed, and will require to be shifted in a very short time.
The large cutter and jolly boats very much worn, and not fit to repair.
Several of the timber-heads forward and abaft decayed and wanting to be replaced.
A new fore cap.
The knees of the main deck beams wanting to be new bolted.
Several of the chain-plates wanting to be shifted.
In my opinion His Majesty's armed tender Supply will want, in the course of another year, a total repair, and which cannot be done in this country conveniently."

On the 15th March, 1791 Lieutenant Ball wrote to Mr Stephens:

"I beg you will please to inform their Lordships that herewith I have enclosed the state and condition of His Majesty's said armed tender under my command for their Lordships' inspection, and with all due submission to their Lordships, I beg to say the Supply will be very much worn by the time she can be got to England, should it please their Lordships to order her to be relieved.

I likewise beg to acquaint you, for their Lordships' further information, that the repairs his Majesty's armed tender will require in another year can't possibly be done in this country, there being no shipwrights, as well as the very badness of the timber, which is not fit for decks and topsides.

I am to request you will please to moove their Lordships to allow me to return to England for the benefit of my health (having laboured under a violent illness for these several months past, and my life greatly despaired of) should it not please their Lordships to relieve the Supply from this station...

The violent and shocking putrid fever which raiged on board the Supply at Batavia, and since we were there, has graitly impaired the constitutions for almost all the officers and men of the Supply that I much fear they will not get re-established in this country. And pray you will, as well for myself, please moove their Lordships to have them likewise relieved..."

The fact is that this sturdy little ship and her crew had been overworked and subjected to excessive strains for a very long period. When David Blackburn took command of her, she must have been in a shocking condition. When he sailed her in on the 22nd March, 1791, she was most probably unseaworthy.

In June, 1791, a month after her return, Collins wrote:

"The bad weather met with by the Supply during her last voyage to Norfolk Island had done her so much injury, that, on a careful examination of her defects, it appeared that she could not be got ready for sea in less than three months. In addition to other repairs which were indispensable, her main mast was found so defective, that after cutting off eighteen feet from the head of it, and finding the heel nearly as bad, the carpenter was of the opinion that she must be furnished with an entire new mast. This, when the difficulty of finding timber for her foremast (which, it must be remarked, bore the heavy gales of wind she met with, as well as could be desired even of wood the fittest for masts) was recollected, was an unlucky and an ill-timed want; for, should it happen that supplies were not received from England by the middle or end of this month of July, the service of this vessel would be again required; and, to save the colony, she must at that time have been dispatched to some settlement in India for provisions. She was therefore forthwith hauled alongside the rocks, and people were employed to look for sound timber fit for a mast..."

That was in June, 1791.

But the following September, on the 24th, two carpenters, J. Boyd of the *Gorgon* and R. Reid of the *Supply*, signed a report on the condition of this little ship. Having listed the defects, they wrote:

"It is our opinion, from the above stated defects, that the Supply is in the greatest want of a thorough repair which we think cannot be done in this country. We are further of opinion that a slight repair can be given her here, in the course of three months, with what assistance we have at present, to enable her to run six months longer. And we do further declare that we have taken this survey with such care and equity that, if required, we are ready to make oath to the impartiality of our proceedings herein."

On the same day a Mrs Parker wrote:

"We found lying here His Majesty's armed tender the Supply, with her lower masts both out of repair; they were so bad, that she was obliged to have others made of the wood of the country, which was procured with great difficulty, several hundred trees being cut down without finding any sufficiently sound at the core."

So the little *Supply,* surely one of the bravest ships ever to grace any fleet, at last left Port Jackson for England on the 26th November. She had done her duty in a way that will enshrine her as a ship to remember in the saga of the seas. Both Collins and Tench expressed their feelings at her departure. They would miss her and they expressed themselves well.

Collins wrote:

"The services of this little vessel had endeared her, and her officers and people, to this colony. The regret which we felt at parting with them was, however, lessened by a knowledge that they were flying from a country of want to one of abundance, where we all hoped that the services they had performed would be rewarded by that attention and promotion to which they naturally looked up, and had an indisputable claim."

Tench wrote:

"The Supply, ever the harbinger of welcome and glad tidings, proclaimed by her own departure that ours was at hand... It was impossible to view our separation with insensibility—the little ship which had so often agitated our hopes and fears; which from long acquaintance we had learned to regard as part of ourselves; whose doors of hospitality had been ever thrown open to relieve our accumulated want, and chase our solitary gloom!"

It was all very understandable. Only those who had gone out in her—or in the rest of the First Fleet—knew exactly what this gallant little ship had come to mean to them. From an inanimate object, a collection of timbers and canvasses, she had become nothing less than a link with home, soaked with sea-spray, weathered by sun and wind, made wise by a thousand hazards, she had become a character in her own right — as much part of the history of Australia as those who sailed in her — or who watched her come and go with their hopes and fears.

As to those who sailed in her — Collins was right. They had an indisputable claim to promotion, recognition, and reward if ever any men had.

But David Blackburn, even though he commanded her on two important occasions and was always in a high position of authority above deck; even though he had Governor Phillip's own recommendation to their Lordships at the Admiralty — received no such promotion. Like the ship itself he went home very much the worse for wear, worn out by over four years' service. Less than three years later he was dead.

CHAPTER FIFTEEN

Notes Concerning Final Letters and The Death of Blackburn

IT IS March, 1791 and in the little settlement of New South Wales there is, once more, a positive ferment of letter writing.

From the Governor downwards everybody is committing to paper thoughts, facts and figures — many of which are to form the tangible history of early Australia.

Many important despatches are being prepared; the state of the Settlement and its needs are being graphically depicted; and in many a letter there is revealed more than a hint of the desperate situation in which the Colonists find themselves.

David Blackburn himself is already under orders to command H.M. Armed Tender *Supply* by reason of a directive from Governor Phillip signed on the 19th March. But he does not actually sail until the 22nd March and we find him occupying his time in the completion of other letters home.

One was to his friend Richard Knight, and this is now in the possession of the Mitchell Library, Sydney, (see Appendix).

The second letter, the original of which is before me as I write, was to his sister in Norwich. It really consisted of two letters — both despatched together. (see Appendix).

It will be seen that he began this letter on the 12th August, 1790, and that he added to it on the 17th March, 1791.

These two dates alone must give us some idea of the utter loneliness of life in the Colony. Probably most of us have had the experience of starting a letter on one day and finishing it days, weeks — or perhaps even months later. But here is a man far from home — with enough news to fill a book — so aware of the complete absence of any practical means of communication — that a letter commenced in mid-August does not get completed until the following mid-March — and then only because of the knowledge that a ship is about to sail for home.

As will be seen, the first part of this letter was written in Batavia — the *Supply* having gone there on an urgent mission for supplies. The second part is written in Port Jackson immediately prior to sailing in Command of the *Supply* on the 22nd March, 1791.

This letter, with a great mass of precious correspondence from Port Jackson, was crossed to England in the transport *Waaksamheyd* (a Dutch Snow). This vessel had come from Batavia, having been hired there by Lieutenant Ball from a Mr N. Engelhard at very exorbitant rates — the total, including cargo and hire amounted to £11,688. 6. 9d. considerably more than Blackburn's stated figure. In fact, when the *Waaksamheyd* reached Port Jackson, her Master, no doubt acting on instructions from the wily Dutch owner, offered to sell the vessel to Phillip for £6600 with all her furniture and provisions. This offer was refused, though it ought to have been accepted.

In the end the ship was hired for a voyage to England at the rate of £1 per ton per month. As she was of 350 tons burden and since the journey was likely to take six months, the cost would have been over £2000. Furthermore, if anything happened to the ship the British Government would have been asked for thirty thousand rix dollars — about £6000 — in compensation. It was not a very shrewd business deal on the part of the Governor, especially bearing in mind that, having had no news of the *Gorgon*, he was now without any other ship except the wonderful little *Supply*.

With regard to this letter to his sister begun on the 12th August, 1790 and completed the 17th March following, one doubts whether much more history could be packed so nonchalantly into a letter home! Between these lines we see the first Settlement with its horizons limited to an area of 70 miles by 70 miles, oblivious of both its own future and the future of the great continent on which it is based; we see famine casting its shadow over events; the notorious Major Ross sent out of the way to Norfolk Island; an expedition in search of provisions; the wreck of the *Sirius;* the emergency voyage to Batavia and the discovery of Ball's Maidenland, Tench's Island and Prince William Henry Island; we see the Dutch East Indies in 1790, handkerchiefs from Spitalfields for sale in Batavia; David Blackburn to-ing and fro-ing between Port Jackson and Norfolk Island — this time in command of the *Supply*. We get pictures of New South Wales, Norfolk Island, the produce and the natives —

often with a surprising economy of words. For instance, speaking of the natives, Blackburn writes:

"They would be great thieves if they had but pockets."

Or again:

"Mr Ball's health not permitting him to go to sea, the Command of the Supply was given to me till his recovery and I sailed on the 23rd January, 1791 and performed the voyage in 5 weeks and brought the whole of the Sirius's ship's company, 91 persons."

Nothing very flowery about this! No mention of difficulties, no mention of risk, no mention of the deplorable condition of the little *Supply*. Just a few swift lines conveying information that was to become part of Australian history.

*   *   *

Apart from the letter that he wrote to Richard Knight two days later, the letter to his sister, completed on 17th March, 1791, was the last letter of David Blackburn to survive relating to his voyage to or from Australia. There is one other surviving letter written on the 17th September, 1793, from London. It is addressed to a Mr Richard Harper at Plymouth Dock. In it he asks for certain of his possessions to be sent to him at Chatham as he had been appointed to H.M. Ship *Dictator,* Captain Dodd. (see Appendix).

We can however, continue to track down the fortunes of our friend for on the 8th January, 1795 the following letter was addressed to Mrs Mary L. Blackburn at Mr Burrows', Magdalen Street, Norwich.

Union Hall, 8th January, 1795

Mrs Mary L. Blackburn,
at Mr Burrow's,
Magdalen Street,
Norwich.

Madam,

In answer to your favour of yesterday I am to inform that I received a letter from your brother Mr D. Blackburn on the 24th ultimo dated on board the Dictator at Portsmouth the day before, since when I have not had the pleasure of hearing from him. I have sent him your letter by this post and I believe the Dictator will be shortly paid off—she lays at Portsmouth for that purpose.

> I am Madam,
> Your most obedient Servant
> R. Robertson.

Then on the 3rd February, 1795 comes the final news. It came in the shape of a letter from Lieutenant Thomas Pamping to Mrs Blackburn and it read as follows:

From Lieut. Pamping to Mrs Blackburn
London February 3rd. 1795.

Dear Madam,

I sit down with heart felt sorrow to inform you of my old friend, your son David's decease. He died a few days after our arrival at the hospital (Haslar). I did suppose as I had informed Mr Robertson of it that he had acquainted you in this but this day seeing him and find on enquiry he had not done it, caused me to put pen to paper on this disagreeable subject, as there was a particular friendship between himself and me.

Prior to his decease he made me acquainted with all his business and the manner of disposal of all his property on board of which Mr Robertson is acquainted. The greatest part of wearing apparel he left his servant, a very good attentive boy. For all this business I shall account to Mr Robertson. I am in possession of his last accounts current with him and also his ticket for what money he has in the funds. Have also delivered him his journals for the recovery of his wages during this last voyage. I would wish to know as soon as possible, as those papers are of consequence, whether I shall enclose them to you, or deliver them to Mr Robertson. Your answer dear madam, per return, will much oblige me, as after so disagreeable a voyage I am going in the country to see my family.

Hoping you will be enabled to bear this stroke of unhappiness with fortitude, of which my poor friend had a great share, I remain,

> Madam,
> Most respectfully,
> your most obedient servant,
> Thos. Pamping, Lieut.

Please direct for me at No. 12 Betts Street, Radcliff Highway, London.

The death of her brother was a severe blow to Margaret Blackburn, especially since news of it came after a long period of silence — a silence made all the more inexplicable by reason of his obvious affection for home and family. What exactly happened we shall never know. All we do know is that he died of consumption in Haslar Hospital (Portsmouth) — worn out by his endeavours and privations.

And this, too, we know for certain. In spite of Major Robert Ross and other preposterous bullies like him who were to make their presence felt in later years, the First Settlement contained great men like Watkins, Tench, Captain William Hill and notably of course, Governor Phillip himself whose resolve and high-minded purpose kept things steady during those years of turmoil.

And to their names must be added that of David Blackburn — a quiet efficient Englishman who did his duty and received for it precious little reward.

That he gave himself unstintingly cannot be doubted, and but for a few letters home to his sister in Norwich all that he did towards the foundation of Australia would be forgotten.

CHAPTER SIXTEEN

The Final Adjustment

IT WAS a June morning in Itteringham when the letter came. Nearly four months had gone by and at first I hardly noticed the envelope among my post. But it registered at last — The Lord Howe Island Board.

It read as follows:

Lord Howe Island Board

> Chief Secretary's Office
> 121, Macquarie Street,
> Sydney.
> 8th June 1973.

Dear Mr Neville,

Further to our previous correspondence concerning the re-naming of Rabbit Island I am pleased to inform you that all official steps have now been taken and Rabbit Island henceforth will be known as Blackburn Island. Likewise Rabbit Island Passage has been re-named Blackburn Island Passage.

I am sure that this news will give you immense satisfaction and I am looking forward to the provision of a seat to be installed on the Island with a suitable inscription. May I suggest, however that, as Rabbit Island is only visited infrequently by tourists that a more appropriate positioning for the seat would be on Lord Howe Island itself (on Flagstaff Hill) which is in very close proximity to Blackburn Island.

The Board would appreciate your views on this aspect together with advice as to your proposals concerning the subject seat. Your interest in this matter has been very much appreciated.

> Yours faithfully
> (sgd.) K. W. Thomas
> *Secretary.*

Only the Australians could have done this so quickly. Over here, in Britain, such a matter would have been tossed from bureaucrat to bureaucrat for years. But there, in Sydney, they had held their meeting, listened to the evidence fairly—and then, I imagine, somebody had said: "Well, I suggest we do something about this. Fair's fair. This Englishman deserved his name on the map." And, everybody concurring, they had *done something*. Bingo! Just like that!

Oh, we may be older in Britain, with more tradition behind us. We may have history as long as your arm—but we have a lot to learn from the straightforward, direct methods of great people like the Australians.

*   *   *

Later that morning, I looked out at the river which flows under the old mill house in which we live. I looked at the water, sparkling and alive, and without effort my mind travelled back across nearly two hundred years to that day when the *Supply* anchored for the first time off the coast of Lord Howe Island. The 12th March, 1788.

"...Having seen the colony settled in their tents, on the 9th in the evening, took leave of them and now steered for our new discovered island which we made on the 12th. and anchored in the large bay on its south west side and at 4 in the afternoon displayed the English colours on shore and took formal possession of the island in the name of his Brittanic Majesty. Lieut. Ball then named the different parts of the island... There is one large bay and two small ones on its south west side. The two small ones he called Callam Bay, the name of our surgeon, the other Hunter Bay after Captain John Hunter of the Sirius, the large bay Prince William Henry Bay and a small green island nearly in the middle of it Blackburn Isle..."

A sense of great joy stole over me.

After lunch, I thought, I will go and see Joe Dawes about making the seat.

CHAPTER SEVENTEEN

Completion

THE village of Corpusty lies about two and a half miles from Itteringham, so it did not take me very long to get there.

I found Joe Dawes in his workshop amid the clean smell of wood and sawdust. There was a frightful noise from some machine or other and it would have been difficult to have made myself heard in the ordinary way. Add to this the fact that Joe has been stone deaf since the age of ten, and it will be seen that my position was impossible. So I wrote a note and handed it to him. It said somewhat ambiguously, "May I have your wife?" Joe smiled with that wide "I love the world" smile of his, put down his work, and came with me to my car.

It was less than half a mile to his home and there we found Mrs Dawes to act as interpreter.

We all sat down at a table in the living room, and I began. It must be borne in mind that they knew nothing about the book or anything connected with it so there was a fair amount of explaining to do. So I talked to Mrs Dawes and she relayed everything to Joe, using her fingers and her lips.

By the time I came to the matter of the island, I had warmed to my theme, and a bowl of fruit that stood on the oval table helped me to make things clear.

I helped myself to an apple and put it near Joe. "There," I said, "is Sydney. And here," —taking an orange— "is Norfolk Island, nine hundred miles N.E."

Joe was beginning to look bewildered and when a tomato appeared mid-way between the two, as Lord Howe, and a box of matches next to it as Blackburn Island, he began to eye me warily. But it all became clear to him in the end and when I produced the letter from the Administration Board, he quickly became enthusiastic.

Could he design and produce a really fine seat? I asked — though I knew the answer well enough already. Joe smiled enigmatically, got up from his seat, and fetched a box of coloured slides.

We held them up to the light and saw pictures of the wonderful work through which he has gained his reputation.

There were free-flight geometric stairs, curved staircases, carved portraits, and exquisite pieces of furniture. He talked to me about them in that strange high-pitched voice of his. A stranger cannot always understand what Joe is saying. He has had to learn the meaning of sound through struggle and groping over the years. But he always gets there in the end. And the nearer you are to him, the more you enter into the being of Joe—the more you understand.

Joe Dawes is a Yorkshireman. He is forty years old and has two children aged ten and thirteen. I first met him when I gave a talk to a Round Table meeting and I never forgot his face, and the way it broke into beauty when he smiled. In his silent world, unimaginable to any of us, try as we might, he had faced suffering squarely and had beaten it, squeezed joy and laughter out of it—and all this had gone into his eyes, into his whole face. He is a man you can never forget, once you have met him.

He had moved into Norfolk twelve years before "because the grass looked greener". And in spite of his severe handicap, he has already achieved greater success than most in his work with wood. With the City and Guilds of London he holds a first class cabinet maker, full technological certificate and an advanced pass in furniture design and furniture materials. He has a diploma in timber technology and is an associate of the Institute of Wood Sciences, for which he did research in polyvinyl acetates. His abstract carvings have been on exhibition at Norwich Maddermarket Theatre, the Aldeburgh Festival and in London.

Before I left him he had already begun to think about the prevailing temperatures and climatic conditions on Lord Howe Island and I smiled to myself as I climbed in my car and set off for home. There wasn't a man in the whole of England I would sooner entrust with the commission.

*   *   *

It took a long time, of course. English oak wasn't good enough for him. It had to be Norfolk oak and it took some finding. It had to be seasoned. It had to be cut into suitable strips in Norwich.

He brought me drawings that he had made, but a year went by before I even saw a piece of the wood.

Then, at last, it came and when I went over to his workshop, there he would be, standing among the shavings, shaping and planning.

Back at Itteringham, we announced the project and though I hadn't asked the people of England before, I asked them now. And the people responded. They gave their coins, sometimes their banknotes, sometimes their cheques. A Trust Fund was set up and the £600 we needed was over-subscribed. In fact, we received £608.35. I found it a revelation to discover how many people had relatives in Australia. And let this be said to any Australian who may read this book. There is a bond between our two countries that can never be broken — let the politicians and the economists say what they will. We are one people and we shall remain that way until the world has overcome her growing pains.

So, at last, the seat that Joe Dawes had made came to Itteringham Mill where it was assembled and where it remained on exhibition from July through to September.

"This seat" it said, "was given by the people of England in memory of David Blackburn, Master of H.M. Armed Tender Supply, who sailed with the First Fleet to New South Wales in 1787 and after whom Blackburn Island was named on the 12th March, 1788".

The rains of Norfolk fell upon it and the sunshine of Norfolk shone upon it — just as in the old days before when the great tree grew somewhere in the County. Quite possibly, this very wood was being fashioned out of the elements before Lord Howe Island had even been discovered! Visitors sat on it, had themselves photographed on it, patted it, and stroked it. And on the last day of September, Joe Dawes came, took it to pieces and helped to put it on a lorry belonging to Consolidated Transport. We all stood and watched it trundling down the long drive until it was out of sight — starting its long journey to Sydney and thence to Lord Howe.

Jean Brearley, my kind correspondent from Lord Howe Island, was born there and her mother and grandmother, too, her ancestors having settled there from Sydney in 1854. She wrote:

"Flagstaff Hill is a very popular site, especially when the flying boat is landing and taking off, as folk go to watch this spectacular event, as it is quite close to the landing base."

Of course, they have stopped the flying boats now, and an air-strip has been built on the island. But this makes little difference. In the years to come, when Lord Howe has become one of the most popular tourist resorts in the New South Wales territories, a great many Australians will look out from our seat across to Blackburn Island. They will have read the inscription on the front and perhaps some of them will think back to the days when a handful of devoted men founded a great nation.

APPENDIX I

All existing letters written by David Blackburn, fifteen of them, are published here for the first time. I am greatly indebted to the Mitchell Library, Sydney for permission to use the five items they hold and where this has been done, full details are given. The remaining letters were loaned to me by Tom Grix and but for his kind co-operation, this book would not have been possible.

1. **Letters written prior to the sailing of the First Fleet on 13th May, 1787.**

Black Bull,
Bishopsgate.   12th March, 1787.

My dear Sister,

I arrived in town safe and just time enough to see my friend Chadd before his departure for the coast of Africa and went down to Woolwich with him in a post chaise to join his ship which he expected was there. But she had been sailed for the Downs two days before — so he must post chaise it all the way to Dover. Tom is in good health and his wife very forward in her pregnancy but I do not know when she expect to be laid aside. P. is certainly deformed his right breast is too far forward and his left shoulder too far back. They say he is very ill tempered but he was very good with me and pleased with my nursing him. I was astonished to hear her say she did not believe it was her own child. I found him sitting on a stool with his arms pinned behind him, no wonder he is fretful, but the moment his mother released him he came to me and would not quit me till I went away.

At the Navy Office I find I stand 226 on the list consequently cannot come on the half pay list yet, but am high enough up to be called to service and Chadd advises me to write to the Navy

Board which I think I shall do but will first see Martineau and ask Mr Henslow's advice. Captain Anniss is not yet arrived in town but is expected every day. Tomorrow I shall call on the gentleman Mr Barrow mentioned. I was two hours to-day enquiring for Mr Viney but could not find him. I shall go to lodgings on Thursday on Friday but whether at Deptford or in Clare Street near Temple Bar I am at present uncertain. I delivered all the letters safe and had a quarter of an hour's chat with Mrs Calthrop, she is a much finer woman than I expected from the recollection I had of her as a girl. I shall expect to hear from you in the week. Direct your letter to the Bull. I hope my Mother's forehead is getting well and that you continue drinking porter and regaining a good constitution.

Elsmere is at Gravesend therefore I shall not see him. Mr Baker says that he believes your letter can be sent to Newbury the latter end of this week but if he has no opportunity of sending it then I shall send it by the Post this day sennight. I shall write to you again in the week if anything occurs. If not shall wait for your letter. Give my duty to my mother and love to sister Betsy and love to Rand when you see her—and don't forget to finish my watch cushion.

Your affectionate brother D. Blackburn.

Mr Fancetts,
No. 14 Craven Buildings, London.   4th April 1787.
My dear Mother,

In my letter to sister Betsy I said I was promised employment in a few days in the Navy. I was then in hopes of being appointed to the Bulldog sloop of war but was sent for to-day to the Navy Office and informed that a warrant is made for me appointing me Master of His Majesty's armed store ship Supply bound to Botany Bay now at Portsmouth and will sail in a few days. I did all in my power to decline accepting of this offer, but am told that I *must* go, unless I mean to throw myself entirely out of the Service. I am therefore to receive my warrant tomorrow and I suppose shall be ordered to Portsmouth immediately—I hope my chest is on its way to London. If so, brother Tom will forward it immediately to Portsmouth. If it is not, you had better send it by one of the coaches and write

Tom word where and when it will be in London, for I am afraid they won't let me stay long enough in London to receive your answer to this.

I am a good deal vexed at this voyage as I am by no means prepared for it, especially on such short notice — I want and must have more clothes, linen particularly. I must buy books, charts, etc. for the south seas, but where the money is to come from I know not, unless you can and I'm afraid you cannot, supply me with 10 pounds. My agent will advance me as much more when I receive my warrant, which would do pretty well, provided I get my chest in time which I am very much afraid of — if we should sail without it I shall be badly off indeed. You will write by return of post to me and direct to Mrs Fancett's who will if I am gone send your letter after me to Portsmouth and you had better write by the same post to Tom, that he may know how to forward the chest to me — it is not certain how long we shall be gone, whether two or three years, — but I will let you know more about it when I know more myself. I will write again tomorrow and let you know when I leave town and how to direct to me at Portsmouth. Give my love to sister Betsy and believe me your ever

dutiful son,
D. Blackburn
in haste.

London. 6th April 1787

My dear Sister,

I have to-day received a letter from sister Betsy which informs me you are to be in Sudbury as to-day. I therefore write in haste to tell you I set out tonight for Portsmouth to join my ship now laying at Spithead and bound with the rest of the squadron to Botany Bay. I have been at a great deal of trouble in endeavouring to get my warrant for her changed but nothing can effect that. Mr Henslow assured me that if I refused to go in her I should be struck off the List and have no claims to employment till every other master had been provided for by rotation and that the Navy Board considered it as a particular mark of their favour to employ me so soon. She is a brigg and I shall be paid only as a sixth rate viz. £5 per month, which of itself is a hardship as I have passed for a third rate which is £7 monthly. Aunt Martineau has lent me £10 which is very acceptable. I have purchased a dozen new shirts, a coat, 6 pairs of shoes, a dozen pairs of stockings, some charts of the East Indies and South Seas and hope I shall go to sea tolerably well stocked.

The Brigg—her name is the Supply, is commanded by a Lieut. Ball, an old ship mate of mine in the Victory. I hope we shall be happy together and I know some other officers who are going out in other ships, they talk of sailing every day but Mr Henslow says he does not think they will sail these ten days as the lawyers have not yet finished a Code of Laws for this New Establishment.

I cannot say I am very fond of the voyage and am vexed that I shall be deprived of the happiness of seeing you again before we sail. However, you will write to me often, and direct your letters for me Master of His Majesty's Armed Tender Supply, to be left at Mr Lads at the White Hart, Point Street, Portsmouth.

I have time to write no more at present, but that I am your most affectionate brother D. Blackburn.

D. Blackburn,
Mr Lads,
White Hart,
Point Street,
Portsmouth.   10th April, 1787.

I received your letter my dear sister this morning and the watch cushion safe in it, which be assured and I will preserve whilst I have life, at least till we see each other again, which I don't despair of. Do not therefore my love let your affection for me deprive you of the fortitude you are mistress of, but rather look forward with a cheerful hope of a happy meeting on our return, remembering that the same providence which has hitherto protected me in all my dangers is still the same and that the southern hemisphere is like this equally under his allseeing eye. I confess it is not a voyage I should by any means have chose, but I must go or be struck entirely off the List. It is therefore my Duty to obey without murmuring and I shall make it my study to go through my Duty with cheerfulness. I have but one wish and that I am afraid is impractible which is that I should see you here on your way to Newbury, it would not be above a guinea and a half more expense and I can spare that for so desirable a satisfaction.

It is not known when we shall sail but it is supposed about the middle or latter end of this month. My chest arrived here yesterday, it goes on board tonight and tomorrow I go on board myself. I went on Board on Sunday with my Captain, who was very civil and as far as I can judge at present seems to wish to live with me on friendly terms. If so, it will take off a deal of the unpleasantness of so long a voyage.

I believe we are to stop at Teneriffe for wine and also at the Cape of Good Hope for livestock and from thence proceed to Botany Bay and it is generally supposed we shall be gone three or four years. It is a fine climate and I dare say a healthy one and every officer who returns from this expedition will certainly be provided for by the Admiralty and Navy Boards; it is said that there will be other ships sent after us in less than a twelvemonth, if so you will have an opportunity of writing to me by them and when we arrive at the Cape of Good Hope, I shall certainly write to you.

I have packed up my nieces things in a deal box and directed them to Brother Tom and they set off tonight for London and I have wrote to him by this post to inform him of it. You will write to me by return of post and let me know whether I may expect you here. Mrs Lad (Miss Allcock that was) will accommodate you to your wish and I shall be on shore to receive you.

Give my Duty to our dear Mother, I shall write to her tomorrow. I have not time tonight. I wrote to Betsy yesterday. Remember me to Laetitia when you write and to her brother and family. My love to Little Bet.

God bless you my love and believe me your most affectionate

Brother, D. Blackburn.

Supply 15th April 1787

I received your letter my dear sister yesterday but could not get the answer on shore time enough to save the post. In your letter you have said enough to convince me that it is not essentially necessary for you to come to Portsmouth and that seeing you again before I sail could not be to any advantage to either and the objections you mention, particularly your cold, has put it out of my power to wish you to take the journey. We must therefore content ourselves with thinking of each other till my return. There will not, believe me, one day pass without a wish for the health and happiness of my best beloved sister. With your letter I received one from sister Betsy and one from Richard Knight with a long postscript from Laetitia, filled with good wishes and prayers for my welfare. I will write to Devizes before we sail, our time is yet uncertain.

I have been on board ever since last Wednesday and am upon good friendly terms with Captain Ball and it shall not be my fault if we don't continue so. The vessel I am in is small and rather uncomfortable, but if we are happy amongst ourselves that will not much signify—you will continue writing to me. Let me know when you expect our mother will join you in your road to Newbury, else I shall not know how to direct to you, but if we are not sailed when you and our mother arrive in London, your cold better and she should express a wish to come to Portsmouth with you, I hope I shall then see you. Let me hear from you by return of post.

> Believe me,
> Your ever affectionate brother,
> D. Blackburn.

Direct to me as before.

Supply 19th April 1787.

I received your letter my dear sister yesterday but was not able to answer it by return of post as it blew fresh and we lay five miles from Portsmouth. I am truly sorry that by what I wrote in my last you should think I am hurt by your objections to coming to Portsmouth. Be assured my love I am not, they are rational. I know your affection for me is too strong for me to doubt it. Your cold was of itself a sufficient cause with me for your declining the journey—believe me my dear sister, your health and happiness are as dear to me as my own and I am very happy to hear that your cold is better.

We hear to-day that the Governor has settled all his business in London and is expected here this week. If so we shall sail in a few days after his arrival. It will be impossible for me to get leave of absence any further from the ship than Portsmouth, even if you were now in London, and I relinquish my wish of seeing you here, for great as the pleasure would be in seeing you, there must come a parting painful to us both.

I am on very friendly terms with my Captain and dare say we shall continue so and my dislike to the voyage begins gradually to wear off. We are to stop either at Madeira or Teneriffe and from thence round the Cape of Good Hope where we shall wood and water and take in cattle and from thence proceed to Botany Bay. It's supposed it will be January before we arrive there and that our voyage will take up three years at least.

You will write by return of post and let me know when you proceed to London and whether brother Tom has received Betsy's cloaths as I have never heard from him since I sent them.

Give my love to the dear little girl. I received sister Betsy's letter and answered it, give my love to her when you write to Norwich and my duty to our good Mother. You have not said whether she is in Norwich or with you. I shall write to her as soon as I receive your next. May health and happiness attend you prays your sincerely affectionate brother,

D. Blackburn.

Supply 2nd May 1787

I received yours of the 22nd of last month in due time and to-day have one from sister Betsy which I shall answer by this post which is the first time these seven days that I have been able to get a letter on shore for the blowing weather we have had. However, I hope this will find you and our mother in good health and spirits at Lambeth from whence you will write and let me know when you shall be at Newbury.

I am glad you have accepted Brother Thomas's invitation. You don't say how my niece does, I hope she is well. The time of our sailing is quite uncertain, though we expect it every day, but it is generally believed we shall not sail before the middle or latter end of this month. I know of no means for you to convey letters to me, except by such ships as Government may appoint hereafter, which it is supposed they will do yearly. My leaving a letter or attorney would be useless as my personal pay cannot be through till I return and then no one can receive it but my agent, whose name is Benjamin Robertson, a clerk in the Navy Office.

I am in haste to get this letter on shore to save post, therefore must leave with my hearty wishes for your health and happiness and duty to our mother and subscribe myself your ever affectionate brother,

D. Blackburn.

Supply 2nd May 1787

Write by return of post.

I wonder I have not yet heard from brother Thomas, it is now a fortnight since I wrote to him.

Portsmouth 6th May 1787

I received yours my dear sister this morning and am indeed truly concerned at the death of that good man, the father of your Laetitia. I would write to Devizes by this post but am at a loss to express my sentiments upon paper on such an occasion, but I will write soon, tomorrow if I can. I am of your opinion that Laetitia cannot wish you in Newbury so soon and yet I think if my mother and you were with them you would at least by partaking of their grief, lessen it. However, I shall hear by return of post what Laetitia's wishes are and consequently how to direct to you for our stay will be very short now, as Captain Phillips who is going out Governor of Botany Bay is arriving in Portsmouth this evening and it is thought a week will be the longest of our stay if the wind permits, the whole fleet are ready for sea at a day's notice. We for our part have two years' provisions of every species on board, wood and water excepted and you will be glad I know to hear that my Captain and I continue on friendly social terms and I dare say we shall continue so. Indeed tis his interest to be civil to me, as I am the next in rank to himself and except the surgeon, who I think is a good man, a little younger than myself, he has no one else to converse with but me and in case of sickness of his side, the command of the tender must devolve upon me and I am not without hopes of being a gainer by this voyage, tho' no prizes can be taken, for the Lords of the Admiralty have promised in printed instructions to us, that our assiduity in following these instructions will recommend us to their particular notice and favour, these instructions principally tend towards accurate observations and remarks on the different coasts, harbours, etc. we may meet with in this pretty voyage, and it is supposed that we being a small vessel are to be employed surveying the coast of New Holland on that side where we build our fort and land the convicts, which will take a year at least to make a chart tolerably sufficient for the press and I have well stocked myself with paper, books and proper instruments for the purpose.

I am not surprised at poor Parlow's death and with you thank God for taking him to himself. I am sorry my mother is so much fatigued with the journey but hope a few days' rest will perfectly recover her health and spirits.

In consequence of yours this morning when I came on shore I soon found by enquiry that my box had been arrived three days at the Inn here, but not delivered to Mr Lad's. However, I have got it safe with the letter it enclosed for which I thank brother John. Give my love to him and Mrs B. I wish her safely out of her present situation and believe me my dear sister

your most affectionate brother
D. Blackburn.

Portsmouth 6th May 1787

It is not clear to me that you understand how I am situated — the Armed tender is a Brig. not commanded by a Captain but a Lieutenant, therefore no Lieutenant under him — the Master next — then Surgeon — Boatswain — Gunman — Carpenter — therefore I am second in Command on Board and as tis known that my Commander Lieutenant Ball is to be made a Captain the first opportunity I think I stand an equal chance of preferment. My pay at present is £5 per month.

Adieu.

Supply 9th May 1787

My dear sister,

I have but just time to save the post to inform you that Friday is the day fixed for our sailing if the wind will permit. I am and shall be very busy all this night and tomorrow, fear I shall not have time to write to our mother but sending affectionate duty to her and hope she will write to me by return of post.

I need not say how much I wish your health and happiness nor how sincerely I am your affectionate

Brother D. Blackburn

I will if possible write to Sister Betsy and Mr Knight tomorrow. I need not put you in mind of writing for I am sure you will by return of post.

2. Letters written during the outward journey.

Supply, Teneriffe — St Cruiz.
June 5th 1787.

My dear Sister,

I know it will give you pleasure to know that we arrived here safe and in good health on the 2nd of this month after a passage of three weeks from Portsmouth and that we have a prospect of compleating our long passage to New South Wales without any malignant distemper amongst the convicts as they are not now confined in irons or kept below the decks, under certain restrictions, except such as are refractory, etc. In general they are all in good health and spirits.

We are to take in water and wine here and shall sail in a few days for a Portuguese settlement called Rio Janeiro, in South America, where we shall get wood, water and refreshments, and from thence proceed to the Cape of Good Hope where we shall be I suppose in about October from whence you shall hear from me again if possible. From thence we have a long track of ocean to pass, no land being in our way till we make the coast of New South Wales. It is totally unknown to us, at least to me, how long we shall remain there but it is generally thought we shall be employed surveying the coast harbours, etc., at all events I don't think we shall be home in less than three years.

I am sorry I had not time to write to Devizes before we sailed. Do you my dear sister, thank Mr Knight for his letter to me and your Laetitia for her postscript which I shall keep in the purse till I have the pleasure of seeing you and them again.

I am sorry I did not get a letter from our mother before I sailed but we sailed in such a hurry at last that I dare say I missed her letter but by one post.

Give my duty to her and my love to sister Betsy and Thos. May God bless you my sister with health and happiness.

Your ever affectionate brother
D. Blackburn.

H.M. Armed Tender *Supply*
2nd Sept. 1787.

Rio Janeiro on the coast
of South America in
Lat 22 deg. 54 m. south west
from Greenwich.
Long. 42 deg. 44 m.

I wrote to you my dear sister from Teneriffe by a vessel bound to London which I hope you have received. This will probably be some months before it reaches England as it comes by an English South Sea ship which is put into this harbour to stop a dangerous leak. I hope by this time your health is quite recovered and that you are happy amongst our amiable friends at Newbury or Devizes. Believe me my dear sister that a day has not passed since I left England without a prayer for yourself and your Laetitia's health and happiness and that neither time nor absence can ever abate my love and esteem for you both. I hope our good Mother and sister are well. I have enjoyed a very good state of health and spirits.

I will now give you a short account of our voyage thus far. We sailed from Portsmouth on the 13th of May, eleven ships in all, including H.M. ship Sirius of 24 guns on board of which is Captain Arthur Phillip, Governor of the new colony and his retinue. The Supply of 8 guns, 6 ships with convicts, viz. 596 men and 267 women and three ships with stores, provisions, etc. We had an excellent passage from England to Teneriffe where we lay eight days taking in water, wine, etc., and were supplied daily with fresh beef. We set sail from thence on the 10th of June and directed our course for St Iago, the principal of the Cape de Verd Islands where we arrived on the 19th of June, but as the wind did not admit of our getting to a proper anchoring place without great loss of time, the Governor took in the signal which had been made for anchoring and we proceeded to the southward, crossed the Equator on the 15th of July and arrived at this place on the 6th of August. Here we have refitted our rigging, wooded and watered and taken in a good stock of port wine. This place, which is very little known to the English, is perhaps the most extensive harbour in the world and is well defended by a number of fortifications. The city is large and regularly built; it has 17 principal churches, which are very magnificent besides a great number of inferior churches, chapels and convents. It is governed by a Viceroy from the Crown of Portugal, who is attended with as much state and his palace as grand as any monarch in Europe. The number of inhabitants are computed at 45,000, about two thirds of which are slaves. The rest are Portuguese gentlemen and merchants, who export into Portugal sugar and tobacco and some cotton. But their greatest source of riches are precious stones of different kinds, particularly the diamond and topaz.

I have not seen any curious shells here, but I have got some skins of birds of this country which I think will be worth your acceptance, tho' I fear I shall not be able to procure enough to make a muff.

The officers and gentlemen of the city have given us the highest opinion of them by their repeated civilities and attentions and you can easily judge how comfortable we must feel ourselves amongst such people at the distance of 4,571 miles from England. We have been here now a month and are ready for sea and shall sail in a day or two for the Cape of Good Hope which we hope to make in a month or six weeks, where I suppose we shall stop to wood and water and then proceed on our course to the Eastward for Botany Bay or elsewhere in New South Wales. I shall certainly write to you again, if we touch at the Cape, after which it will be impossible to convey any letter to England till the convict ships return to Europe. They are all very healthy, having in all from their first embarkation buried only 20 men and 2 women and there has been 8 or 10 births, chiefly females. I cannot quit this subject without saying that the health of the convicts may in a great measure be attributed to the humanuty of the Governor, who gives them every indulgence their situation will admit of, none of them are confined in chains or even under the deck by day, except such whose behaviour deserves such punishment and they are constantly supplied with fresh provisions, fruit and vegetables.

It will give you pleasure to know that I am upon friendly terms with my Captain and have no doubt of a continuance of it.

God bless you my best beloved sister. Present my duty to our good Mother, love to my brother and sister, my love and esteem to your Laetitia and her brother. My respects to Aunt M. and all friends in Norwich and believe me,

Your ever Affectionate Brother,
D. Blackburn.

H.M. Armed Tender *Supply*, Cape of Good Hope.

9th Nov., 1787.

My dear Sister,

I hope you have before this time received the letters I wrote you, the first from the Island Teneriffe, the last from Rio Janeiro, which place we left on Tuesday 4th September, and arrived here after a pleasant passage across the Pacific Ocean on Sunday 14th October.

I hope by this time my dear sister's health is perfectly recovered. I have enjoyed an uncommon share of health ever since we left England, and the fleet in general have been very healthy. We have been here now a month, taking in water, and a large quantity of livestock for the Colony, so that could you see the 'Supply', she would put you mind of Noah's Ark, except that we have no woman on board.

We expect to sail on Sunday next for Botany Bay, the distance is near 9000 miles, so that we may expect, if no particular accident detains us, to arrive there in the latter end of February or beginning of March and from thence I will write you again by the ships which will return to England after the convicts are landed, and I do not despair of hearing from you, as we are told that there are one or two ships to be appointed to bring out clothing, etc., for the Colony.

I hope you are happy and still amongst our Newbury friends. You will give my love and esteem to your Laetitia and Mr and Mrs Knights, tell them a day never passes without my wishes for their health and happiness.

Give my Duty to our good Mother, who I hope is well, my love to sister and Thomas and Niece, Aunt M. and family, and believe me my dear sister, your ever affectionate brother,

D. Blackburn.

I have wrote to sister Betsy by the same ship which brings this, she is bound to Amsterdam so that I suppose it will be March before you receive this.

3. Letter from Margaret Blackburn Norwich, 1785

Norwich 3rd April 1785.

I am extremely sorry my dear brother to inform you that through the mismanagement of your brother Thos. your box of things is still in England. I dare say you have been put to considerable inconvenience by this delay but still as so many months have elapsed since we thought you had most probably received them and of course so much nearer coming to England, I think it will be best not to send them at all, at least not till we hear further from you.

In my last I complained to you of his procrastinating spirit, great an evil as that is I wish it could be recorded amongst his greatest faults, but alas he has not had prudence to keep himself within the pale of more imperfections and foibles; I shall not trouble you nor myself with a detail of his irregularities, he is removed from a set of bad companions with whom he got acquainted in London while his wife was in Norfolk and himself is now come down to us — he promises to be good — while he keeps his word he is to remain here and work at Mr Deceaux, the cabinet makers, but whenever he fails, he is to look upon this no longer as a home. This affair of his has put an affectual stop to the plan I have long formed of going out, and my mother breaking up housekeeping — we must now (notwithstanding all the reluctance I ever did and ever shall feel at the thoughts of promoting our income in Norwich) think of something that will answer the purpose; to effect this, nothing occurs to me with the probability of success so much as taking three or four young ladies to board and educate. My mother has consented and will undertake the trouble of the housekeeping part, all the rest devolves upon me. We have mentioned it to some of our friends who give me their flattering approbation of the scheme and hopes of success.

Monday 5th.

I am very much at a loss for a subject with which to bring this up to the respectable size of a letter, what shall I do? To send it in its diminutive state 3000 miles would be infamous; I find no power within myself to enlarge it — I have applied to my mother for assistance which proves but the widow's mite to me, though to you it is a volume of maternal benedictions comprised in the short sentence of "tenderest love to my son" — there now, I have wrote that, I am as bad off as ever, for down towards the bottom of this page I must get by hook or by crook as I always make it a rule with myself, whether I have anything to write about or not to scrawl over two pages when I am writing to *my friends,* to common acquaintances notes are sufficient. Well! I declare it is the luckiest thing in the world for you and me that balloons were ever invented, there is a subject at once for us, you are all out done and beat to nothing, there is not a British tar amongst you can show your faces in a company of modern philosophers, these pretty gentlemen can make their evolutions and manoeuvres in the air with as much address as ever an admiral in the British Fleet, they can fly to the moon in an hour and to the Antipides in three seconds, pray can your Flora sail half so fast? Down with your proud vaunts then, and lower your flag to these *superior* beings, these demi-gods, these knights of Arthur! To the eternal honour of every true English tar, be it known that one amongst them? Vernon (Admiral in the British Fleet) have put to proof his courage (if not his skill) in entering the lists with these adventurers, but alas how poor a figure a man cut when out of his element, the poor Admiral no sooner saw himself elevated some hundred yards above the earth than he felt a trepidation seize him which he confess he had never experienced in the midst of battle or the most tempestuous sea, but his fears were heightened to agony when some of the rigging of this new fashioned vessel gave way, he roared out his commands with such vociferation to lower sail and drop anchor upon the first land they could make; to obey his orders it was first necessary to throw out ballast in order to accelerate

(xx)   Sydney Cove, New South Wales, 20th August, 1788.

(xxi)   Sydney from Hyde Park, 1827.

(xxii)   An early nineteenth century view of Sydney.

SMYTH.

Mansell Collection

(xxiii)   General view of Sydney in 1846.

(xxiv) Circular Quay, Sydney Harbour about 1886.

Mansell Collection

(xxv) Steam tram-cars in North Street, Sydney by Melton Prior, 1889.

Mansell Collection

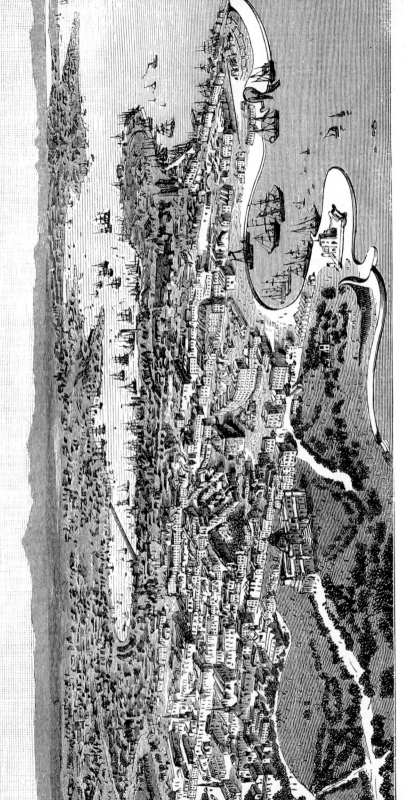

(xxvi)   General view of Sydney, undated.

(xxvii) Bridge Street, Sydney in the late nineteenth century.

Australian News and Information Bureau

(xxviii) Hyde Park near the city centre of Sydney today.

Australian Information Service Photograph by A. Osolins

their ascent into a certain latitude (altitude amongst philosophers) which for a reason better known to them than to the
Admiral or myself, produce a more rapid and easy descent to
terra firma than they could otherwise procure. This apparently
counter operation to his commands so affected the seaman
that he lost his reckoning and descended to earth in a state
more easily imagined than described; in fact the Admiral's
whole conduct was perfectly natural, and what might be
expected from a man who has more courage than philosophy.
He no doubt felt within himself the ability to "dare what man
dare" and "who dare do more is more or less than man," and
however laughable the story may tell, I would first advise these
aerial sprights to walk the quarter deck of a man of war in the
midst of a close engagement, and if they find their feelings
dissimula, or their conduct more heroic than the Admiral's in
their Balloon, then let them triumph in their element but leave
him to do the same in his. But I have not done with balloons
yet, we are going to have an ascension from Norwich by a man
who have actually got his machine here and will take any
gentleman who will give him a hundred guineas up with him
(this is that precious metal gold) squandered away upon every
trifle, while the poor are starving, and poor me pining for a
competent portion of those conveniences that only five times
that sum would procure me for life. My dear sailor, adieu,
without 5 shillings in my pocket, or 5 grains of wit in my pate, I
am happy in signing myself your affectionate sister,

Margaret B.

4. Letters written from Sydney Cove, Batavia and Norfolk Island.

Supply — Sidney Cove.
Port Jackson 12th July, 1788.

Miss Blackburn,
St Michael's, Coslany,
Norwich.

My dear Sister,
     As I wrote to you from Teneriffe, Rio Janeiro and the Cape

of Good Hope, which letters I hope you have received, I shall now give you a short account of our voyage from the Cape to the present time. We sailed from thence on the 13th of November. Met with contrary winds and sent on but slowly for the first week. The wind then came fair and on the 25th the Governor, a Lieut. King and Lieut. Dawes, came on board the Supply and we made all sail for New Holland, leaving the fleet to follow us under the care of H.M. Ship Sirius. We had a very quick but windy passage, and made Van Diemansland, the south part of New Holland, on the 3rd of January 1788, having run in 50 days the distance of very near 6000 miles. But it was the 19th before we arrived at Botany Bay, where we anchored at 4 in the afternoon, all in good health and on the 21st the rest of the fleet arrived. The next day, the Governor, Captain Hunter, the Master of the Sirius and myself, went to examine a place where Captain Cook supposed (to have landed) and there was a harbour to which he gave the name of Port Jackson. We found it an excellent and extensive one and on the 25th returned to Botany Bay and conducted the whole fleet up the harbour to the place where the camp and storehouses now stand. It is about 6 miles from the entrance. The Governor has named it Sidney Cove. In the beginning of February, we took on board six months' provisions, with the necessary implement for settling a colony on Norfolk Island, discovered by Captain Cook and on the 14th sailed with Lieut. King as Superintendent and Commandant of Norfolk Isle, a surgeon a midshipman, a master weaver, with 9 men and 6 women convicts. We were soon overtaken by a very severe gale of wind which continued till the 16th but did us no damage, and on the 17th we discovered an island, to which we gave the name of Lord Howe Island. As the wind continued fair, we put off an examination of this island till our return. We arrived at Norfolk Isle on the 29th of February but it was the 3rd of March before we were able to land, which we did with the utmost difficulty, but found it would be impossible to land the stores and provisions there as the sea broke with great violence on the shore. We therefore went in search of a better place which I discovered by going in a boat to the south end of the island where on the 6th and 7th we landed the colony with all their stores and provisions safe. To this place, Lieut. King gave the name of Sidney Bay.

This Colony is settled here with the idea of cultivating and improving the flax plant and cutting down fir trees with which the island is covered and grow to an amazing height and size. Some of them measured 27 feet round. This island is about 15 miles round. It is in general surrounded by inaccessible rocks and high perpendicular cliffs on which the sea breaks with such violence that landing is always difficult and very often impractible. Having seen the colony settled in their tents, on the 9th in the evening, took leave of them and now steered for our new discovered island which we made on the 12th, and anchored in the large bay on its south west side and at 4 in the afternoon displayed the English colours on shore and took formal possession of the island in the name of his Brittanic Majesty. Lieut. Ball then named the different parts of the island. It is about 6 miles long and about 2 wide. At its south east end are two very high mountains which he named Mount Gower and Mount Lidgbird, the valley between them Erskine Valley. There is one large bay and two small ones on its South west side. The two small ones he called Callam Bay, the name of our surgeon, the other Hunter Bay after Captain John Hunter of the Sirius, the large bay Prince William Henry Bay and a small green island nearly in the middle of it Blackburn Isle. I was on board whilst this ceremony was performing, or it should have been called Knight Isle. The island is uninhabited but we found plenty of the finest turtle I ever saw on the beach, some of them weighing upwards of 500 pounds. The bays abound with excellent fish and the island with pigeons, a kind of quail and some other birds peculiar to the place. But no running stream of fresh water that we saw. We took on board as many turtle as we could conveniently stow and made sail for Port Jackson where we arrived on the 20th March. The turtle were an acceptable present to the Governor and colony. We have been since at Howe Island and are now preparing to sail with the fresh supply of stores and provisions for Norfolk Island. We really know so little of New South Wales that it is useless to attempt to describe it.

The Land in general is very rocky and small spaces of clear ground. Our gardens have produced nothing worth notice, nor I am afraid will not whilst we remain in the colony which I hope will not exceed two years. The natives are black, they are quite naked and very dirty and are to all appearances most miserable wretches — they live in caves and hollow places in the rocks and so far as we know have no other food but fish and fern root. They almost always go armed with spears, very long and barbed at the end with a fish bone. We have never yet been able to persuade them to come in to the camp or on board the ships, tho' they frequently pass and once three canoes came alongside the Supply but would not come in, nor will they eat or drink with us nor taste any of our food. They seem to be a harmless in-offensive people but like all savage nations are cunning and will always sooner or later revenge an injury. They have killed a convict and wounded another who were in the woods collecting herbs, but we have every reason to believe they were the agressors, indeed the convicts in general are a set of most abandoned wretches — four have been hanged for breaking into and robbing the officers' tents. We have never seen above 40 of the natives in a body but once. On the 6th of June, a party of gentlemen with their servants and 4 soldiers walking to Botany Bay met with a body of 300 of them all armed with spears and targets. However, they did not attempt to disturb our small party but let them quietly pass. On the 4th of June, His Majesty's birthday was kept here, the Sirius and Supply fired 21 cannon each at sun rise at noon and at sun set. All the officers of the Navy and Army dined with the Governor who then named the adjacent country round Port Jackson, the County of Cumberland. On the 22nd of June at 20 minutes after 4 o'clock in the afternoon a shock of an earthquake was felt on board the ships and through the camp. Our surgeon and me were then in the woods about a mile and a half from the camp and were at that time standing still and silent examining some gum running from a large tree. The shock was an undulation from south west and did not continue I think more than two seconds of time. It was accompanied by a noise like a distant cannon. The trees shook as if a gale of wind was blowing. The afternoon was remarkably clear and a very light breeze at N.N.E. I have enjoyed very good health since we left England and I think this climate a very healthy one. There has been but 50 buried since our arrival here and as many marriages and 26 births. It is said that some ships will be sent to us next spring. If so I hope I shall hear from you and my friend Knight to whom I have wrote a fuller account of our voyage than I have time to do now.

I hope my good mother is well and that yourself and sister Elizabeth established in health and spirits. Perhaps you are still among our worthy friends at Newbury or Devizes and I hope you are because I know you must be happy there. I hope your Laetitia is in good health and happy. I beg you will make my love and respects to the family. My duty to my mother, love to Eliza, brother and little niece and respects to our friends at Norwich. Adieu my dear sister and believe me your ever affectionate

brother
D. Blackburn.

Supply, Sydney Cove,
Port Jackson,
New South Wales.   15th November, 1788.

I wrote to you my dear sister by the last ships which sailed which was in July last, of which this will be little more than a duplicate, for I think we know at present very little more of this country than we did then. The country as far as it has been penetrated affords but a bad prospect to the new colony. It is a continued track of swamps and rocky hills covered with a thin loose soil. A mixture of sand and black mould. Our gardens have produced little or nothing, the young plants spring up very quick but soon after pine away and die. I believe the Governor's is the only garden which has as yet afforded a few vegetables for the table. There is now some wheat and barley which promises to do well, if the small animals of the opossum kind and the ants (of both which here are great numbers) do not destroy it. The valleys abound with cabbage trees with which most of the houses are built for the present and several stone buildings are begun. The Governor's house will be a very elegant one and is near finished.

I believe I told you in my last that the town will be called Albion and that it is in the centre of the county of Cumberland. The trees of various kinds grow to a great size but when sawn into plank the wood is short, heavy and not fit for house or ship building. In my opinion the only recommendation to this part of the coast is the excellent harbours of Port Jackson and Broken Bay which is about 12 miles further North—Port Jackson is perhaps the finest in the world. There is high land to be seen at the distance of about 40 miles inland where perhaps the soil will be better than so near the sea and a detachment from the main body is intended to be settled there as soon as possible. We have been here now above nine months without being able to persuade any of the natives to live or associate amongst us, or without being able to learn a sentence of their language—they seem to be the most miserable of the human race, they go quite naked and are very dirty. Their principal food seems to be fish and a few roots. Many of the men want the left fore tooth of the upper jaw and some of the women have the first joint of the left little finger cut off, but what these particular marks of distinction are intended for I know not. They have canoes of the most simple construction, being nothing but the bark of a tree about 12 feet long, tied at each end by a kind of running vine which grows near the seaside. In one of these wretched canoes a man, his wife and a child will go up and down the harbour striking fish with a spear, at which they are very dexterous. If they are hungry they do not wait to dress their fish but eat it raw, or if they take it on shore to dress it it is thrown on the fire, scales, guts and all, warmed through and eat. They live in caves and hollows of the rocks with which the coast abounds and sometimes they make a nest of the leaves of the cabbage tree just big enough to sleep in. The men go armed with lances of about 12 foot length pointed with a sharp fish bone, a very dangerous weapon, with which they will kill at 30 or 40 yards distance. They have clubs headed with stone and stone hatchets. They have lately been very troublesome to our fishing and foraging partys, have wounded several and killed three, so that we have been obliged to fire among them and are now always obliged to go well armed as they have several times come down in a body of 60 or so and thrown stone and spears at us whilst fishing and even attempted to take the fish from us. They seem to have no curiosity, for they will scarce take off their attention from fishing in their canoes whilst a ship has to pass close by them in full sail. They appear to have no mode of worship or any religious ceremony that we can perceive. They burn the bodys of their dead and scratch a little earth over the ashes. They are great thieves and are very angry if prevented from taking what they have a mind to and in all probability will always look upon us as enemys and take all advantages in their power.

There are several extraordinary animals in this country, the kangaroo is very curious, some of them have been killed of 200 pounds weight and are very good eating, they have four legs but in making their escape they use only the hind with which

they hop with great swiftness over the high grass and under-
wood, so that it is with great difficulty a good greyhound can
overtake them. The forelegs are short and small and only used
in scratching up roots, etc., for food. The tail is very large and
strong and is their principal weapon of defence and with which
they would soon break the bones of the strongest dog. They are
of the opossum kind and have a false belly in which the young
remains whilst sucking and into which it retreats in time of
danger. They bring forth young not bigger than a mouse and
we have often shot old ones with young in the belly as big as a
rabbit. There are several small species of the oppossum, flying
squirrels, dogs, not unlike our fox dogs—some snakes which
seem to be harmless, numbers of ants, some very large which
bite very severe. A beautiful variety of birds and of fishes, none
of the last are quite like those of the same class in Europe but
partake of the likeness of two or more different kinds and in
general their colours are very brilliant. The torpedo is frequently caught and its numbing quality is indeed very powerful,
especially when the fish is first taken. The sea abounds with
whales of a good size and sharks, the largest I have ever seen.

As the surface produces little of value to us so it is supposed
the internal parts of this coast will afford us nothing worth
digging for—a slate quarry is found but the slate is too brittle
for use. It is the opinion of many that iron may be found here
and I am of the same opinion. But of the purer metals I think
none can be expected, at least on this low part of the coast.
However an artful fellow (a convict) found means during the
absence of the Governor (who was gone with a party inland) to
raise a report that he had found a *lost mine,** on which an
officer and guard was sent to be conducted by him to the place
but he gave them the slip, was soon after taken and confined
till the Governor's return when, after much equivocation and a
good flogging he owned that he had filed a guinea and a brass
buckle and mixed the filings up with a quantity of earth, the
glittering particles were easily perceptible and when tryed by
fire of course actually produced a little gold. He said he hoped
by this scheme to get his freedom, but I am since informed that
he now denies all that he said then and still says he knows

---

*"A convict came back with wild tales of gold, but he was accused of having
manufactured the gold out of a shoebuckle and was flogged." *Australia—Her
Story,* Kylie Tennant.

where the place is but will not tell. Since I wrote last we have been in the Supply to Norfolk Island, with six months' provisions for that colony and about 2 months ago I was sent by His Excellency with the ship which brings this called the Golden Grove, under my Command to Norfolk Island, with an additional number of male and female convicts, stores, etc., and two years' provisions. I have been returned but a week and on my passage back discovered part of a very dangerous ledge of rocks about 130 miles to the Eastward of Lord Howe Island. Of what extent these rocks are I know not for they reached to the North East further than could be seen from the masthead. I brought with me a small cargo of deals of timber and small masts and some flax. Norfolk Island is a beautiful spot and bids fair to be a valuable acquisition to the Government. The soil is rich beyond description. Every seed they have sown (except onions) grows as fast as in Europe and they have already several acres of ground laid out in gardens. The island is about 17 miles round — it is a continued range of hills and valleys covered with most beautiful pine trees fir for the mast of the largest ship. Some of them measure from 30 to 40 feet and upwards in circumference and from 100 to 180 ft. in height. The wood is of a much finer and closer texture than the mats we get from Russia. The flax plant grows all round the sea coast in the greatest luxuriance so that cordage and cloathing cannot be wanting. There are few animals on the island, chiefly rats, some pigeons and paraquets. The sea round it abounds with fish and turtle is caught in plenty during the summer months from November to March. Near the middle of the island is a hill higher than the rest of the island called Mount Pitt from which issues springs which run in different directions and form rivulets which water the whole island. It is much to be regretted that this island affords no harbour or place of safety for ships and that landing is almost always attended with great difficulty and danger on account of the violence with which the sea dashes against the shore which in general is steep and rocky. A midshipman and 4 men were drowned in a boat the last time we were there in the Supply, though the sea was then apparently smooth.

The only two remaining ships of our fleet sail for Europe tomorrow, so that we shall now be very solitary these six months to come, unless some ships arrive from England as we cannot expect the Sirius (which sailed for the Cape of Good

Hope on the same day I did for Norfolk Island) in less time. I hope you will miss no opportunity of writing to me, I shall expect a large packet by the first ship by which I hope I shall hear you are in good health. Give my love to Sister Bet. I hope she will write also. You will let our friends at Newbury or Devizes know that they have constantly my best wishes for their health and happiness. The few days I spent in that little family will ever be remembered with pleasure. I hope in another year Government will think of relieving us, believe me I begin to think the voyage a long one.

Give my respectful duty to our good mother, who I hope is well. Compliments to Aunt H. and family, D. Columbine, etc.

Your most affectionate brother
D. Blackburn.

5. **Letter from David Blackburn to Richard Knight dated 12th July, 1788 (ML. A6163) (Royal Australian Historical Society:** *Journal and Proceedings.* **Vol 20).**

The *Supply* in Sydney Cove, Port Jackson, 12th July, 1788.

Dear Sir,

In some measure to atone for not answering your very friendly letter before we sailed I beg your acceptance of the following short account of our voyage to this time, as far as I was an eye-witness for information by officers of priority in this fleet. We sailed from Spithead on the morning of Sunday 13th May 1787 and bore down channel with a fair wind. The Supply very deep-laden with stores, which as we met with some blowing weather made us rather uncomfortable and being constantly wet H.M. Ship Hyena accompanied us clear of the Channel and on the 20th left us we being one hundred leagues from the land. The irons were then taken off all the convicts (such only excepted as had behaved ill) with permission to come upon deck and take the air whenever they pleased during the day the weather was now of the wind fair. On the 31st May we passed the island of Teneriffe where the greatest dispatch was made to water and get refreshments for the fleet which detained us there six days. The town of Santa Cruz is the capital of the Canary and subject to Spain. It has a small fort at each end of it and a few straggling guns behind it. The town makes a very decent appearance from the ship in the bay. About a mile from it but when in the town it looks very shabby. The only good building is the church. Here we got every necessary refreshment except fruit which was not in season but wine very cheap and good if their market is held in the middle of the town. The inhabitants a few excepted they are very poor. Their military force is small, consisting chiefly of natives except the Governor and a few officers who have their appointments from Spain. The day before we sailed a convict made his escape from the ship he was in by cutting a small boat from her side early in the night and got on shore unseen. However, a party of marines were sent on shore in the morning by the Governor's permission who found him about nine miles from the town concealed in a cave. We sailed on Sunday the 10th and by the fairness of the weather were gratified with a sight of the famous (?pitre) of Teneriffe distinct and clear of cloud which set our happiness. It stands on the top of a very high mountain snow lay round the foot of it but its top is clear and looks like brown rock with deep furrows in it. At sea it has a very sublime appearance and I am informed that the adjacent coast of Barbary can be seen from the summit to the distance of one hundred and fifty miles or more. We directed our course to the Cape Devard Islands and on the 19th June the signal was made to anchor in Praya Bay on the island of Saint Iago but there being a light breeze of wind there was little probability of getting the fleet to anchor that night. The signal taken down and we proceeded towards the equator which we crossed on Sunday the 15th July and on the 2nd August saw the Coast of Brazil. The fleet in general remarkably healthy and on the 5th the whole fleet got safely into the harbour of Rio Janeiro. This is a remarkable fine harbour and little known to the English or I believe any other nation but the Portuguese who are the possessors. It is governed by a Viceroy who with the officers are appointed from the Court of Portugal. There we had great attention and respect paid us. One reason for it is that Captain Phillip our Governor of New South Wales was a Commodore in the Portuguese Service and much approved of there having I am informed rendered some special service to that Crown. The harbour and town is very strongly defended. The entrance of the river is about a mile and a half wide which is defended by a strong fort built in the solid rock. At the foot of the very high hill on the top of which is a battery of three very large cannon. About a mile within the entrance is a small but strong fort on a rock entirely surrounded by water and about another mile further up is a strong fort on an island at a little distance from the city. But the principal strength of the city is a very large fort on an island at the north end of the city, the cannon mounted on it are very heavy. Immediately after anchoring, permission was given for us to go on shore and be provided with every refreshment.

The city is a mile and a half in length and about a mile in breadth. The streets stand at right angles with each other, are paved by broad flagstones, footpaths on each side. The houses lofty and in general well-built but wooden lattices to all the windows, they having no glass. Their houses are but in-differently furnished but their churches, chapels and mona-steries and convents to the number of seventeen are very magnificent, and their shops are well stocked with an excellent assortment of European goods. The landing place is at a large square before the Viceroy's palace. To the left is a negro market well stocked with poultry, fruits and vegetables of every kind. The palace is a building two storeys high. The upper part appropriated to (?). The lower part is a guardhouse and armoury. Their military force consists of two troops of horse of thirty men each, one regiment of artillery for six hundred men and five regiments of infantry of eight hundred and twenty-one men each exclusive of officers, forming in the whole a body of near five thousand men besides a very numerous militia. Every regiment takes the guard in rotation to the number of three hundred men who are constantly going round and on Sunday they have the addition of horses on account of their slaves being then at liberty and the officers guards and mounts every day at the pattica. The military have entirely the command the meanest soldier having it in his power to control the first inhabitant. Strangers are not allowed to go through the city without a sergeant or corporal after them except officers in their uniform. They are remarkably strict upon foreign ships as no trade is allowed to be carried on but by their own. Their trade consists of sugar, rum, indigo, Brazil wood, whalebone, oil and spermacetti, bullion, diamonds and topazes. The mines are a hundred and fifty miles up the river and very rich. The diamonds are of the finest sort but not large. It is almost impossible if not entirely so to procure admittance to the mines so strict a guard being kept.

The fleet being watered and provided with every necessary refreshment sailed on Tuesday morning the 4th September, saluted the port as we passed it with thirteen guns which they returned. We lost sight of the continent of South America that night and directed our course to the Cape of Good Hope which we made on the 13th October and that afternoon anchored with the whole fleet in Table Bay. All very healthy. We saluted the town next morning with thirteen guns which they returned and the fleet began watering immediately and were soon complete. The town is called Cape Town. It is built of stone and brick and the houses whitewashed on the outside the windows and doors in general painted green. The streets are very broad and stand at right angles but not paved which renders walking very disagreeable in windy weather the ground being light and sandy. The inside of their houses are very neat their furniture much the same as ours with the addition of two shining brass spitting boxes at each table as smoking tobacco is the first thing they do in the morning. The landing place is a wooden wharf built on towers and carried a hundred and twenty feet into the water. It is very strong and high on account of the great sea which sets into the bay into the winter which they reckon from the 29th May to the latter end of August during which time they suffer some of their own ships to remain in the bay. In the end of the wharf are six cranes for loading or unloading vessels and four cocks for watering shipping. In the middle of the wharf is a guard, a gate and wicket which is always shut at dark and all boats are then obliged to go on board or moor to the wharf and deliver up their oars, masts, sails, rudder etc., to the guard who returns them next morning at daylight. At the inner end of the wharfs is the custom house where two officers constantly attend and examine everything that passes. They are very strict, not suffering any but trifling things to pass without leave from the Governor. In case of the arrival of a large fleet a contractor is appointed by the Governor to supply them but single ships are supplied by any principal merchant. Their market is a very poor one consisting of bread, a few vegetables, oranges and some tobacco which they sell very dear. Indeed articles of every kind are at an enormous price. We were much deceived in our hopes of procuring many articles here cheap such as tea, china, hankies and coffee. Better could be bought in England and much cheaper. Their beef is tolerable. Mutton very good and the fat sheep are remarkable for their large flat tails, a lump of solid fat which serves for butter and candles weighing from 8 to 16 pounds. At the end of the wharf stands an old fort of little use now but to hold the Dutch India Company troops about three hundred men. Close to this fort is the place for the execution or punishment of criminals. It stands on rising ground, a low wall round it which you ascend by steps. On the inside is a house where the officers by going it is possible to see the punishment properly executed. Near this place is an hospital, soldiers' barracks containing at present a regiment of Swiss who have not yet been relieved since the late war and these have been the principal defence of the Cape against Commodore Johnstone. The town runs for these barracks about a mile in length and a half a mile in depth. At the back part of the town are the Company's gardens in the middle of which the Governor resides. The only entrance is by a very handsome stone gate where two sentries always attend. Any company whether inhabitants or foreigners are admitted to walk in them at pleasure. Indeed it is the only comfortable and pleasant walk at the Cape. From the gate goes a broad gravel walk in direct line about a mile in length on an easy apart a row of lofty oaks on each side the walk whose tops join and form an arch and behind the oaks hedges of myrtle. At the upper end is the aviary and some dens of wild beasts. They at present consisted of a beautiful tiger cat about 3 feet high, two large wolves, a most mischievious and fierce animal, a large and very ugly baboon, a very beautiful zebra, some foxes and two tartrolls, two dens were preparing for lions with which the interior part of the country near the Cape abounds, also a variety of curious and beautiful birds particularly the ostrich, barbaric crane and birds of paradise.

The inhabitants of the Cape consist of Dutch merchants from Holland and the native Dutch. Their servants are Dutch, their slaves are Malays, African and Madagascar Indians. The whole include upwards of five thousand — the gentlemen here take very little exercise, most of their business being carried on by their clerks and servants. At the west end of the town is a new fort very strong consisting of two bastions of ten guns each and joined by a long wall in the form of a crescent on the top of which is a battery of nineteen guns with embrasures. At the bottom for as many more. At our arrival here their militia was embodied which happens annually. They consisted of 150 horse and 266 foot. The 20th October was the last day of their performing their exercise this year. On this occasion the principal inhabitants were assembled as spectators. The ladies dress in the most fashionable London taste with the addition of some beautiful black and white ostrich feathers in the head and left side of the waist. The gentlemen were chiefly on horseback, the ladies in carriages. Apparently made in England — the exercise is very differently performed. I have seen forty sailors fire a much better volley and it was with the greatest difficulty the horses could be kept in a line. There are no taverns or inns. The custom is for gentlemen to live at a merchant's house as part of the family for which they pay worthily about two dollars equal to twelve shillings sterling not including wines and etc. which together with the washing for which they charge sixty pence a shirt and make living on those very expenses. However they live well and supper is always served up hot and in greater quantity than dinner. The weather here is very unsteady. I have seen from daylight to noon as great a variety of winds and weather as ever I saw. The prevailing winds in the summer are from the east south-east which is directly from the high mountain above the town and is called the Tableland on account of its rising almost per-pendicularly to a great height and being flat on the top. When any strong wind in this direction begins the clouds come pouring with vast rapidity over the top of the mount where they meet a calm (in consequence of the perpendicular form of the land) and fall down like an extensive cataract to about one-third of the way down where they are met by an eddy wind which forces them upwards again till they join the prevailing winds a very curious sight to any person unaccustomed to high and perpendicular land. Being amply provided here we took on board the provisions for the line, stock intended for the colony and bulls, cows, horses, mares and colts, sheep and hogs. The signal for sailing was made on Sunday 12th November but calm prevented our sailing till next day when we went to sea with a south-east wind and stood off those. We made but little progress the first week but on Wednesday the 21st November when we were about three hundred and forty miles distant from the Cape and the wind came fair at north north-east and we pushed the fleet on very fast and on Sunday the 25th Governor Phillip attended by Lieutenant King of the Navy and Lieutenant Dawes of the Marines came on board the

Supply ordering the fleet to follow in two divisions, the three fastest sailing ships together and the rest of the fleet under the convoy of Captain Hunter of H.M. Ship Sirius. We have previously taken on board from the different ships some useful convicts principally carpenters and joiners. At noon we made all sail and left the fleet and on Monday lost sight of them. From this time we had a continued fair wind from north-west to south-west the latter sometimes very strong and consequently raised a very high sea and for twelve or thirteen days we ran at the rate of 130 miles a day. It is remarkable that the wind during so long a run should never come to the eastward nor ever remain more than thirty hours at one quarter but shifted suddenly from one quarter to the other. On the 2nd January 1788 we met with a violent gale of wind at north which lasted for twelve hours and made a most tremendous sea and ended in rain and lightening (the day before we had seen a small land bird flying round the ship) the wind now came to south-west and we pushed forward with all sail and next day Monday the 3rd at 10 in the forenoon made Van Diemans land in the southern extremity of New Holland, the latitude of 43° 37 south, the longitude 146° 56 east from Greenwich and distant from the Cape of Good Hope 5087 miles. After making the land we met with contrary winds, various rapid currents retarded our progress along the coast which we saw little of till the 19th January on which day at 4 in the afternoon we anchored safely all in good health and spirits in the long wished for Botany Bay. The natives as we sailed in came down the edge of the cliffs making a noise and lifting up their spears. Immediately after anchoring the Governor accompanied by some officers went on shore on the north side of the bay and met some of the natives on the beach. We went towards them singly which as soon as they saw a very old man walked from among them to meet him. This man (who probably remembers the dress of Captain Cook's Officers' clothes) did not show the least signs of fear or distrust. The Governor put some red cloth above his neck. Gave him some beads and other trifling presents with which he appeared very pleased. The natives however soon withdrew to the woods and our party returned on board. The next day we landed in different parts of the bay, saw the natives who came to us without fear armed with spears but without any appearance of hostile intentions and they received anything from us but we could not then get either to

143

drink or eat with us. I went to an elderly man put a piece of blue cloth round his neck and a string of glass beads round his arm shook him by the hand which he seemed to take as a mark of confidence. I pulled a biscuit out of my pocket, broke it, ate part of it and gave him the other piece. He took it put it to his mouth and appeared to be eating and soon withdrew towards his companions. I followed at a small distance. Saw him throw down the bread which I took up unseen by him and found he hadn't tasted it. The next day morning the first three ships of the fleet arrived and on the next day the 20th the Sirius and remainder of the fleet arrived and anchored in the bay all well. The next day the Governor Captain Hunt and the Master of the Sirius and myself went to examine an opening about twelve miles north of Botany Bay where Captain Cook supposed there was a harbour to which he gave the name of Port Jackson. We found it perhaps as fine a harbour as any in the world with water for any number of the largest ships. There we stayed for two days examining the different little bays or coves with which the harbour abounds. One of which about five miles from the entrance to the harbour the Governor fixed upon and to which he gave the name of Sydney Cove and we then returned to Botany Bay and on the 25th sailed with the Governor in the Supply for Port Jackson and next day the whole fleet followed and in the evening all anchored safe at Sydney Cove. Time was then busily employed erecting the tents, landing the provisions, soldiers and convicts. In the meantime *we* were taking on board provisions and the necessary implements for establishing a colony on Norfolk Island. Discovered by Captain Cook and on the 14th February we sailed from Port Jackson with Lieutenant King, a surgeon and midshipman from the Sirius, a weaver, nine men and six women convicts with the wind fair which in two hours increased to a violent gale and continued to the 16th but did us no damage. On the morning of the 17th we discovered an island at a great distance and the next day sailed within four miles of it. As we were undoubtedly the first who had ever seen it Lieutenant Ball named it Lord Howe Island. As the wind was then fair we made the best of our way towards Norfolk Island which we reached on the 29th February but it was 3rd March before we were able to land which we then effected with the greatest difficulty but found it would be impossible to land the stores or women on account of the violent seas which broke on the shore. We therefore went in search of some other spot with little hopes of success and on the morning of the 6th I was sent in a boat to explore the south coast part of the island and found an eligible place for landing and the next day we landed all the colony there with their provisions stores etc.; to this place, Lieutenant King the Superintendent and Commander of Norfolk Island gave the name of Sydney Bay. This island lays in 29° 02 south latitude and 168° 10 east longitude from Greenwich. It is about fifteen miles in circumference and its steep shores rise almost everywhere perhaps perpendicular to the height of eighty or a hundred feet above the sea which is sixty feet deep within a quarter of a mile in general round the island and the sea lashing its rocky shores in a terrible manner which renders landing impossible even in Sydney Bay when the sea is much agitated. The appearance of the island is certainly beautiful from the sea. It is covered with the tallest and largest pines some of them measuring twenty-seven feet round and were at least fifty feet high before they branched. How high they are above that I cannot say as none were cut down whilst we stayed but I think their tops are more than one hundred feet from the ground. There is a small rivulet of fresh water at Sydney Bay but no grass that saw fit for cattle.

The island rises towards the north end to a high hill which Mr King has named Mount Kitt. On Sunday the 9th March having seen the little colony settled in their tents and rendered them every assistance in our power we at 4 o'clock that afternoon weighed anchor and directed our course towards Howe Island which on the 12th we saw at a distance of sixty miles and next day anchored in a bay on the south west side. The island lays in the form of a crescent. It is about six miles long and one mile broad. At its south end stand two very high mountains covered at the top with cabbage tree and shrubs. Indeed the whole of the island abounds in the cabbage and mangrove. The island these two mountains excepted is moderately low.

A light sandy soil and no running stream of fresh water that we saw. However it could be a valuable acquisition to the colony at Port Jackson for it abounds with turtle much superior to any I have ever seen. On the shore we caught several sorts of birds particularly a land fowl of a dusky brown about the size of a small parrot a bill four inches long legs and feet like a chicken. Remarkably fat and good plenty of pigeons and white fowl something like the guinea hen with a very strong thick and sharp pointed bill of a red colour stout legs and claws. I believe they are carniverous. They hold their food between the thumb or hind claws and the bottom of the foot and lift it to the mouth without stooping so much as a parrot. Some of them have a few blue feathers on the wing. There is also web-footed fowl. In general of a deep blue its bill two inches long straight but suddenly bent downwards at the end very sharp and strong its tail three inches long. It does not seem formed for a long flight having only six long feathers in the wing. Its breast is covered with very thick and long down which grows from the tips of very strong feathers with which the whole breast and belly is covered. Its length from tip of bill to tip of tail twenty-two inches. The extent of its wing from tip to tip twenty-five inches. We took them burrowing in the holes like rabbits. The bay abounds in a variety of excellent fish. At 4 o'clock in the afternoon we took possession of this island in the name of his Britannic Majesty and displayed the English colours and Mr Ball named the different parts of the island. The two mountains Mount Gower and Mount Lidgbird, the valley between them Erskine Valley, a large bay near the middle of the island Prince William Henry Bay, two other bays to the left of it Hunter Bay and Callam Bay and an island in the middle of Prince William Henry Bay Blackburn Isle. Had I been present at this ceremony it should have been named Knight Island. We took on board eighteen turtle of near five hundred pounds weight each and next morning we put to sea and directed our course for Port Jackson. About thirteen miles in the south east direction from Howe Island stands a beautiful pyramidical rock which I think is a mile or more perpendicular height and not more than three-quarters of a mile base. To this Mr Ball has given the name of Balls Pyramid. The island lays in thirtyone degrees thirtysix south latitude and 159°04 east longitude and is 389 miles from Port Jackson where we arrived on the 20th March. We have since been at Howe Island but found no turtle the winter being too far advanced. They are all gone to the north into a warmer climate and I suppose it will be November before they return. With respect to this country I am really at a loss my friend what to say. It is true we know but little of it but I believe it is the general opinion that it will be a number of years before the mother country derives any advantage to the expense of maintaining a colony on it.

What little we have seen of it is rocky with here and there a small space and clear ground where the soil in general is a black mould mixed with sand. It produced no wood that we have yet seen fit for ship-building. The trees grow to a great weight and size but most are hollow or decayed in the heart, and the best when sawn into planks are short and brittle. We have never found any fruit except a small berry something like our white currant. A species of the sloe and a bean which grows on a slender stalk which creeps along the ground. Our gardens have produced very little though we had an excellent assortment of seeds, cabbage and turnips, potatoes and onions, some come up very soon but in a few days afterwards they dwindle to nothing. However, some people there who understand farming say the ground is too thick and that in another year by proper management it would be very good. We are certainly at present situated on the outskirts of the country on account of the convenience of so good a harbour. But we have seen on a clear day a ridge of very high land, I suppose thirty or forty miles directly inland. Our parties have never yet been so far but I am informed the Governor intends going with a strong party very early this spring and I think there is reason to suppose he will find much better land there. We have never yet met with any fresh water river nor have I seen but two places on the coast where I think it probable to meet with a river. One of these is about four miles to the southward of Botany Bay. The other between Cape George and Long Nose in latitude 35.22° south which places I hope we shall examine when the summer advances. The animals of this country are all curious. The kangeroo is frequently shot by our parties. It is the only fresh meal they can get. Some of them are very large weighing upwards of 140 pounds. Captain Cook has described their form. I shall only remark that a stout greyhound has little chance of overtaking them. They hop on their hind legs with great swiftness over the high grass. The tail is certainly their principal weapon of defence which they can use with force sufficient to break a bone. The root of a tail of a large one measured eleven inches round and was near four feet long. They have a false belly which is a loose skin which they have the power of expanding or contracting at pleasure. They bring forth the young perfectly formed not bigger than a mouse and in time of pain or danger always take shelter in this false belly. To what age the parent protects them in this manner we do not know but I think not after they are the size of a cat. The flying squirrel is an inhabitant of these woods and two or three animals of the chopurn kind and I am informed some tiny cats have been seen. The natives have small dogs of the fox kind. The birds are in no great number of variety. In the marshy ground some large black swans have been killed differing from ours in nothing but the colour. The woods abound with beautiful parakeets and some cockatoos. The crows are exactly like ours and some beautiful hawks. The harbour is terribly well stocked with fish, some of them very good. The natives are to all appearances the lowest in rank among the human race. They go quite naked and very dirty. They do not seem to live in community but by separate families in caves or hollows of the rocks and as far as we know live only on fish and the root of the fern which grows here in plenty. They dive for fish and oysters with great dexterity. They have canoes of the most simple construction made of the bark of a tree tied together at each end. We have never seen above forty of them in one place at a time except on the 6th June when a party of gentlemen with their servants and four soldiers were walking in Botany Bay met with a body of three hundred and upwards all armed with spears and targets. They did not seem to feel their superiority of numbers but walked out of the track our people were in and let them pass without showing any mischievious intention. There is but one way by which I can account for their being thus collected to such numbers which is that no cannon had ever been fired since our arrival on the coast. (Muskets indeed they had often heard and seen.) Till the 4th June the anniversary of His Majesty's birthday when the Sirius and Supply fired a salute of twenty one cannon each at sunrise midday and at sunset. Probably some of the natives had been spectators from the woods. Might take such a terrible noise as a "dununciation of war" — (he probably meant "declaration") — and were collecting together for mutual assistance. They have since been seen in families as usual in their canoes catching fish and one Sunday three canoes came alongside the Supply but we could not prevail on any of them to come on board. There has been a murder committed by them on a convict who with another was sent into the woods to collect some herbs and his companion was wounded but on enquiry we have every reason to believe that the convicts had been the aggressors from some days before.

For my own part I believe the natives to be a quiet inoffensive people yet I believe they are total strangers to personal fear and have a quick sense of an injury. The convicts (although they have experienced every indulgence from the Governor whose humanity and attention to them whilst at sea and since our arrival here entitles him to their esteem as their best friend) in general are a set of hardened wretches. The tents were scarce set up before they began robbing them. The Governor began with them by trying (after sentence of death had been passed) what lenient measures would do and altered their sentences to transportation on a small rocky island in the middle of the harbour where they were fed upon bread and water during pleasure. But this had no good effect and it was soon found necessary to put the law in full force. Four have been hanged, two more were under sentence of banishment for life but received a pardon on the King's birthday on which day all officers of navy and army dined with the Governor who named the adjacent country round Port Jackson the County of Cumberland. On Sunday the 22nd June at twenty minutes after 4 p.m. in the afternoon a shock of an earthquake was heard through the camp. The surgeon of the Supply and myself were then in the woods about a mile and a half from the camp and were both at the time standing still and silent examining some gum issuing from a large tree. The shock did not last above two seconds. It came from the south-west like the waves of the sea accompanied by a noise like a distant cannon. The trees shook their tops as if a gale of wind was blowing. The afternoon was remarkably mild and serene and very little wind at north north-east. The climate is certainly very healthy. There has been but fifty burials since our arrival — as many marriages. And ten convicts missing. The principal distempers here are the flux and the scurvy both which would soon disappear could plenty of vegetables be procured.

I must now my respected friend finish as the ship which will bring this sails tomorrow. I am afraid you will hardly find it worth the reading. But I was not willing to lose this (perhaps the only) opportunity of writing to you whilst we remained in this country. I hope yourself, Mrs Knight and family are well. I beg you give my respects to your good mother and sister. Believe me you have my sincerest wishes for your health and welfare and when opportunity offers you will be so good as to let my

Newbury friends know that the distance of many thousand miles has not the least impaired the esteem I have for them, I am, yours most affectionately,

David Blackburn.

6. Letter from Margaret Blackburn Norwich, 1789

Norwich September 9th 1789.

My dearest Brother,

Well and happy may this find you, but long, wearisome and uncomfortable must have been the anxiety with which you have expected the arrival of ships from England. I hope the good Captain and ship to whom the conveyance of this and three packets of letters, newspapers, etc., of different dates from me are committed will be favoured by the elements and every possible advantage that can render their passage quick, safe and pleasant. This I venture by post to Portsmouth, willing to give you a chance of hearing as late as possible before the Guardian leave England, that my mother, sister and all our family are in the enjoyment of perfect health and when we heard last from Brother John (which through Mr William Willement to his brother we did about 6 weeks since) he was well in New York and had just received a letter I wrote to him on the receipt of your first letter from Sidney Cove, but John himself have not written to us of many months. You will receive I hope safely, from Captain Riou of the Guardian, three parcels, two written and sent to Portsmouth in hopes of ships going off to you in spring '88. These letters inform you of the journey mother and self took into Berkshire, of the sickness and death of several of our friends, of the state in which we found poor brother Thos., the rapid increase of his threatening symptoms, his going to his old lodgings at Yarmouth to try the efficacy of the sea air and his death there, which happened August 1st. 1787.

My letter of this last spring '89 contains an account of the death of his wife, who died in November 1788 — she kept her house and shop to the last, but was considerably in debt so that not a single guinea, or guineas worth, was left to her dear child Betsy, happily the only surviving one of their children, who upon the death of her mother, immediately came down to us and a sweet child she is. We have changed our habitation, for my Aunt Finche's mental infirmities increased so much upon her, that it became absolutely necessary to keep her in her own room, where our poor sister Eliza, with a steadiness and attachment scarcely credible and absolutely beyond all immitation or precedent, have voluntarily secluded herself from all society or commerce with the world and wholly devote her time and attention in administering every possible comfort and pleasure to the poor old soul, who is totally insensible to everything around her and even the hand that so kindly feeds her, with the pettishness of undiscerning idiotism she beats from her and abuse. In compliance with the wishes of you, myself, Elizabeth and the advice of some others, my mother at length in the latter end of the year '88 consented to go to this house in Magdalen Street, thinking by that means to alleviate in some measure the irksomeness of Eliza's confinement, but as it is voluntary, so it is undoubtedly pleasant to her because she rejects every offer that have been or can be made to relieve her a little and in fact tho' under the same roof, we see but very little of her. She dines with us indeed every day but that is the only time in the 24 hours we ever see her below. The old lady is in fine health and likely many years to exhibit the melancholy spectacle of human nature in ruins.

Your friend Richard Knight was highly pleased and obliged with your letter to him, and in return he wrote you two large sheets full, but sent it to the post office to be forwarded to Portsmouth, but being ignorant of the usual ceremony of paying the postage thro' England for foreign letters, it was stopped in London and when he sent a friend to the general office to enquire for it and pay what was requisite, his friend was told that the letter had been returned to Devizes, but Mr Knight never received it, so no doubt it is totally lost, since I knew that the Guardian was appointed and waiting sailing orders and wrote to him to urge him to write directly and direct it for you to the care of Captain Riou etc., and I think there is little doubt of its getting to him or the care the Captain or any gentleman will take to convey it to you when in his power; we can do nothing more now than wish with all our might for a prosperous voyage to him.

I am afraid you are in wants of many necessaries, your shirts must begin to be thin, coats out at elbows and stockings out at heel. I dare say you are a fine parcel of raggamuffins, if one could but transmute the earth into a transparent map, it would be some entertainment in this land of dress and luxuries, to see the agreable figures yourself and some of your brother officers cut in your dishable, but never mind externals my dear boy, for if your hearts do but remain good and manners not absolutely barbarous, you have still the intrinsic value of the greatest of mankind. I hope the arrival of the Guardian at Port Jackson will be the enlargement of your ship from that station, but it's a long long time to look forward, let winds and waves waft you swift as they will before you can arrive in England.

Richard Knight last week buried his eldest little girl, the rest of the family, Laetitia and mother, are well. We all go in Norwich as usual, Robson is sensible, Rand is pensive, and Willement as gay as ever.

Your mother desires her kindest love and best wishes to you, in which she is joined most sincerely by her daughters, of whom I distinguish myself as your most affectionate sister,

Margaret Blackburn.

7. A letter to his sister
First part from Batavia 12th August, 1790
Second part from Port Jackson 17th March, 1791

It is now my dear sister, 20 months since I wrote to you by the last ships which sailed from Port Jackson, in which my former I believe I gave you but an indifferent idea of New South Wales. I can only now add that it certainly is a very poor country, at least that part of it where the colony is settled. Such land as is cultivated not having produced near so much as the least sanguine amongst us expected. Potatoes and garden stuff however, do tolerably well and the first may in time become a substitute for bread. The best that can be said of the country is the healthiness of the climate and the excellent harbours it affords. At least as far as we have examined the coast. Our knowledge of it does not exceed 60 miles along the coast*and about as much directly in land. The number of acres cultivated is reckoned to be about, besides the gardens of the different

---

*By the 19th March 1791, this had increased to 70 miles by 70 miles. (See Blackburn's letter to Richard Knight.)

officers — the Supply's garden contains 2½ acres and is as good as any. It affords a sufficient quantity of vegetables for the ship's company daily. The country produces nothing of itself on which an European (not knowing the roots which the natives eat) can subsist, and the kangeroo, which are excellent, are now become very shy, so that a constant supply of provisions and clothing will be required for many years to come.

As to the natives, we are almost as ignorant of their particular manners and customs (if they have any) as we were at first. They will not come among us though every method has been used to invite them. We have had some taken by surprise, the first, a man whose name was Arrabanoo, lived with the Governor and was very fond of him. He was of a meek disposition and seemed very contented but for want of understanding him, little was learned from him. He died in about 8 months. Another now lives with the Governor, called Bennelong. He is a merry fellow and does not seem inclined to go away, but no information can yet be got from him for the same reasons. The surgeon general has had a fine boy with him these two years called Nanbarry, he speaks pretty good English but is too young to give any information and it is probable will forget his native tongue, as Mr Bennelong does not like to talk with him, or answer any questions he is instructed to ask, and once struck him. The Reverend Mr Johnstone has a fine girl about 15 years called Abaroo but little has yet been learned from her, tho' she is very fond of Mrs Johnstone. They seem to have no religion. In general they burn the dead.

The Sirius sailed from Port Jackson for the Cape of Good Hope in October 1788 and arrived from thence in May '89 loaded with flour, etc., for the colony which now began to grow short of provisions of every species. However, a supply from England was daily expected but the year '89 ended without any arrival. The situation of the colony became alarming, and in case the expected ships should not arrive, famine without the means of relief was apprehended, the colony was put to a short allowance of such provisions as remained in store and in February a council was held, in which it was resolved that the principal part of the convicts with a detachment of Marines under the command of Major Ross, the Lieut. Governor, should, with their proportion of provisions, go to Norfolk Island and that when this service was performed, the Sirius should be sent to China for another cargo of provisions. Accordingly in March 1790, the Sirius and Supply sailed for Norfolk with about 300 convicts, men and women, and on the 16th, 17th and 18th the people were all safely landed there, also all the provisions from the Supply, but on the 19th the Sirius, in attempting to land more of the provisions was unfortunately drove on shore by the violence of the sea and in ten minutes she was quite a wreck, she went on shore directly opposite the town and thank God no lives were lost. We stayed three days longer at this island, during which time the weater was too bad for anything to be got out of the Sirius. However, I hope as it was fine weather a day or two after, that most of the provision was got from her. Otherwise their situation on the island must be very bad. There is now near 600 people there. On our arrival at Port Jackson we were ordered to proceed to Batavia as fast as possible for a supply of provisions. The allowance of provision at this time was Rice 1 lb., Peas 1 lb., Pork 2 lbs., and flour 2 lb. a week to each person. The convicts were at a shorter allowance. All the boats were employed fishing, under the inspection of proper officers, the fish brought to the publick square and there equally distributed. We sailed from Port Jackson on the 18th April '90 and pursued our course to the Northward and on the 5th of May, discovered land in latitude S. 16 East Longitude which we coasted along till the 9th being then in latitude S.W. 16 East longitude. There is no doubt but we were the first discoverers and Mr Ball has named it Balls Maidenland.

On the 21st May we discovered an island laying in latitude Longitude East. It is not more than three miles round but fully inhabited. Some of the natives came near us in their canoes but could not be prevailed upon to come on board — they were of a lively copper colour and were the largest men I ever saw — their hair was I think cut short but they had all remarkable long black beards which reached down to and covered the whole breast. They seemed very peaceable and had no weapons with them. We threw a large string of beads to them which they just looked at and threw them into the bottom of their canoe. Soon after they all paddled on shore in great haste without any apparent cause, making signs for us to follow them, but we had no time to lose, therefore kept our course. This island is called Tench's Island in respect to a Captain Tench of the Marines at Port Jackson. At 5 a.m. set we discovered and the next day coasted along a very fine island which I believe to be about forty miles in circumference. Some places on it seemed to be rudely cultivated; we saw numbers of the natives on the shore and a great number of very large canoes on the beach but as they did not seem inclined to come off to us we proceeded on our course. This island was named Prince Wm. Henry Island, it lays in Latitude and Longitude East. These islands are in my opinion the Northernmost of a group of islands discovered by Dampier, but he passed too far to the Southward to have seen these.

On the 5th June we made the Northernmost of the Molucca or Spice Islands and had a tedious but pleasant passage through this archipelago and on the 5th July anchored in Batavia Road—this City is the capital of the Dutch in the East Indies. Here we have loaded the Supply with beef, pork, rice, flour and arrack, also hired a Dutch ship of 350 tons burden which is now taking in the like cargo. The expense of this voyage will not be less than £8,850. We expect to sail for Port Jackson in about a week. This is a very fine city, it is built much after the fashion of Amsterdam in Holland, the streets are wide and clean though not paved, they form right angles with each other and have canals running through the middle with a row of trees on each side so that here are a number of bridges. The country for 4 or 5 miles round the city is delightful and the houses of the principal officers and merchants (who all reside in the country and only come to the city to transact business) are like palaces. The number of inhabitants are reckoned 110,000 the greater part of whom are slaves, the number of Europeans are about 10,000, half of which are Creoles or such as are born in India of European parents. The Chinese have the exclusive exercise of all trades, are the only cultivators of the sugar cane and have the management of all their manufactures. As this place is situated only six degrees south of the equator, it may be supposed to be very hot, but the heat is by no means so great as might be expected. It is constantly refreshed by a breeze from the sea during the heat of the day and the land wind which blows all night is very cool. It has always been represented as a very unhealthy place, but it certainly is not so bad, the European merchants who have been resident here many years are instances to the contrary, they look well and live to a good old age and I have no doubt but the malignant fevers which carry off such numbers of European sailors and people of the lower class, are more the fatal effects of hard drinking, bad provisions and perhaps too much fatigue in the heat of the day, than of the inclemency of the climate.

We expected to find the productions of India cheap here, but on the contrary, every article is as dear as in Europe, tea, coffee, and Arrack expected, and I have seen several pieces of silk handkerchief manufactured in Spital fields offered here for sale at about 3s. 6d. per Handkerchief. By the latest news from Europe, Ships must certainly be by this time arrived in New South Wales. If so I hope on our arrival there I shall find a long packet there from you and I hope from Mr Knight to whom I have wrote by the same Packet which brings this. I begin my dear Sister to wish the voyage at an end and once more to visit my native country and be happy among the small but Social Circle of our acquaintance and I hope when we arrive at Port Jackson we shall there find a ship sent out to relieve us and as I am now secure of the half pay when not employed I shall probably feel more pleasure when I see the white cliffs of Albion that ever I did. I hope our good Mother is well, give my duty to her. My kind love to our sister Eliza, tell her I would have wrote to her but as she will see this it is almost needless. You will also give my love to B and sister, Thos, and my little niece and to brother John if you correspond. I have seen several American Gentlemen here and have made enquiries after him but to no effect. Is the good Mrs Knight living? Is your Laetitia, her brother and family well and happy? I sincerely hope they are. You will particularly present my love and respects to them. And let not our other Newbury friends be forgot. My duty etc. to Aunt M and Family — to Dr Columbine, Mr Rand, our good neighbour Barrow family. Above all my dear sister I long to know your situation in life, to know that you enjoy health and happiness would be the most pleasing account I could receive. Adieu and believe me

Your affectionate brother,
D. Blackburn.

Batavia, August 12th 1790.

Port Jackson 17th March 1791

The Packet sailed from Batavia two days before the usual

time by which means I took the opportunity of sending the above.

We sailed from Batavia on the 17th August 1790 and arrived at Port Jackson on the 19th October where I had the pleasure to receive both your packets of letters and papers for which I am much obliged to all the parties concerned, particularly my friend Knight for his long and very friendly letter.

About 6 weeks after our arrival the Dutch ship arrived and we were ordered to Norfolk to bring the officers and seamen of the late Sirius to Port Jackson, in order to their going to England in the Dutch ship. Mr Ball's health not permitting him to go to sea the Command of the Supply was given to me till his recovery and I sailed on the 23rd January 1791 and performed the voyage in 5 weeks and brought the whole of the Sirius' ship's company, 91 persons. They are now preparing for England and will sail in a week. Mr Ball still continues ill on shore and I am to sail in two days again to Norfolk Island with an exchange of officers and troops for that island.

We found everything here as we left it, except that they had suffered by a great drought having had but two slight showers of rain for five months and I believe everyone here is perfectly confirmed in the opinion that this country can never be of any use to the Mother Country — Norfolk Island is indeed a beautiful spot and its soil excellent, but will never be able to supply Port Jackson with corn, therefore of no use. Most of the large fir trees are found to be rotten at the heart and the flax plant grows only round the borders of the island, so that if many hands were employed they would soon want work. I have seen some lines and canvas indifferently made there and if I am to judge of the goodness of the flax by the strength of the lines, I can say but little for either — probably the flax was not properly dressed.

A little while before our arrival from Batavia several of the natives came into the town in a friendly manner, they were well treated — a house of brick was run up for a chief called Bannelong, before mentioned, where his wife, children and relatives often come and stay a day or two, since when many more men women and children are come among us, and are sometimes quite familiar, at other times as shy. They would be great thieves if they had but pockets. They certainly have no

King or supreme magistrate but seem to go in families or small tribes, the oldest man or most expert warrior of which tribe has great authority over the rest. They use their women as their menial servants and sometimes beat them very cruelly, yet they are very jealous of them and never suffer them to be out of sight whilst among us.

They often go out to meet other tribes and fight with them most desperately, the particular reason for which we have not yet been able to ascertain, but among these people who make retalliation an invariable rule, the smallest affront on either side is sufficient to bring on a general battle.

In a box directed to myself, you will find some drawings of birds, plants and fishes of this country, which you may make what use of you please. I have sent three charts of this country to Mr Henslow by Capt. Hunter.

Adieu my dear sister, and believe me
your most affectionate brother,
D. Blackburn.

8. **Letter from David Blackburn to Richard Knight dated 19th march, 1791 (ML A6163) (Royal Australian Historical Society: *Journal and Proceedings*. Vol. 20)**

My good friend,

I wrote you a long letter from Batavia but as I have reason to think it did not reach the packet previous to her sailing (though it was not brought back to me as one to my sister was) I will endeavour to make it up now. For though I am in haste I cannot slip through this opportunity of thanking you for your very friendly letter which I received on my arrival at Batavia and which gave me the pleasing satisfaction of hearing that yourself and family were in good health. May you all long enjoy it and every other blessing.

I have little to say on the subject of this country in addition to what I said in my last. It seems to be the general opinion that it will never answer the ends of Government. On the contrary it will be a constant and heavy burthen on the Mother country. Before this can reach you you will have heard of the loss of H.M. Ship Sirius and that we were sent to Batavia for provisions. We sailed for that place in April 1790 at which time the weekly allowance of provisions to each person was two pounds of flour, two pounds of pork, one of peas and one of rice. The convicts were at a still shorter allowance and even at this scanty allowance the pork would not last longer than the beginning of August. The rice and flour was much decayed and spoiled by insects. By a great drought of river five months the expected crops was ruined and other vegetables parched up. To add to their misfortune very few fish were to be caught though every boat with proper officers were employed on that service the fish brought to the public square and there equally distributed. The situation of Norfolk Island was rather better though there was upwards of six hundred people on that small island; it being the season when immense quantity of birds resort to the highest part of the island to deposit their eggs which are as large as a goose's and I am informed that upwards of 5000 birds have been taken in one night. Add to this they have plenty of onions and potatoes and tolerable crops of Indian wheat.

Our knowledge of this country is still confined to the extent of about seventy miles along this coast and nearly as much of the interior country. A few small spots of tolerable good ground are to be found but in general the country is either immense barren rocks tumbled together in large ridges which are almost inaccessible to goats or a dry sandy soil and a general want of water. I mean rivulets and running streams. When I wrote last the natives were very shy but many of them are since come among us. However we know but little more of them than before. They are certainly the lowest class of human beings. They go in tribes or families, live chiefly on fish, berries and the fern root and where they find most oysters or the best fishing, there they take up their residence in the hollow of a rock till they have cleared the neighbouring rocks of the oysters and other small shell fish which adhere to them and then seek some other place. They are the only people I ever heard of who did not worship some Deity; it is pretty clear they do not — they often come on board our ship which they call an island and are very troublesome for bread which they are extremely fond of. They are very treacherous and however friendly they may appear whilst among us experience has taught us that they are not to be trusted in the woods without an apparent superiority on our side. They throw the spear with great force and skill and will hit a small stick at fifty yards.

We arrived at Batavia on the 5th July 1790, having on our voyage there discovered a tract of land of near four hundred miles long in latitude 10° 52 south long longitude of 162° 30 east which we named Balls Maidenland and two smaller islands which we have called Prince William Henry Island and Tench Island. They lay nearly in latitude 1° 25 south longitude 149° 23 east. These islands are in my opinion the northernmost of a group of islands discovered by Dampier; having loaded the Supply with provisions and hired a Dutch vessel of 350 tons to take on board the like cargo we on the 17th August sailed for Port Jackson leaving the Dutchman to follow us. We arrived there on the 19th October and about six weeks after the Dutchman arrived we were then ordered to Norfolk Island to bring the officers and seamen of the late Sirius to Port Jackson in order to their embarking for England in the Dutch ship and as my Commander Lieutenant Ball's health would not permit his going to sea the command of the Supply was given to me until his health should be re-established. I sailed on the 23rd January and in five weeks returned with all the people of the island who are now embarking and will sail in a few days and I am to sail tomorrow again to Norfolk with an exchange of officers and troops for that island. I assure you my friend I am heartily tired of this voyage and shall be very happy when Government will think fit to relieve us. That time however cannot I think be far distant as we are now near four years from Europe. You would have had a much longer letter with a short description of Batavia and our settlement of Rose Hill about eight miles above Port Jackson but my time will not allow it and I must finish this by begging you will make my respects to every part of your family at home and abroad there are none I love and esteem more.

If you find we are not likely to be sent home I hope I shall have the pleasure of a long letter by the first ships.

I am,
Your affectionate friend,
David Blackburn.

The *Supply*, Port Jackson, 19th March, 1791.
P.S. The enclosed is a kind of a vocabulary which I will thank you to let my sisters see.

With regard to the "Vocabulary" (ML A6163) which Blackburn enclosed, one supposes that this must have been the first of its kind to leave Australia. It is also very probable that it has since been improved upon considerably! But bearing in mind the circumstances under which it was compiled, it is highly commendable that it should have been produced at all!

Natives of New S. Wales	*English Explanation*
Bangia	To Paddle or Row
Brange	Yesterday
Baou bow or bo	The Termination of the future tense of Verbs or a person
As) Ngia Bangabaou	I will paddle or row
Bia	To Bite
Boming	The Redbill (a Bird)
Blowryee or boola	Two
Berang	The Belly
Buya or Kurrabul	The Back
Barrangal	The Skin
Bulbul	The Kidney
Barrin	The Clothing of Young Women
Bunnerung	Blood
Beeanga or Beeang'elly	Father
Bogul	A Mouse
Beeriang	A Bird
Barda	Water
Booroodoo	A Louse
Boodooroo	O
BokBok	An Owl
Bora	A Testicle
Baamoro	Grass
Benelong	The Name of a Man Native
Benelonge	Belonging to Benelong
Beraboong	The Dew
Boong	Posteriors
Birong	Belonging to
Bunga	To Make
Dtooney	A Scorpion
Dtoora	To pinch
Dani or Deeryin Dani	Mine — My Wife
Deeyin	Woman or Wife
Diu Warra	There — or that way
Dargalla	To Scratch
Duralia	A kind of Heron or Bitterne
Dlurrung	The Shoulder
Dedeeai, Dedeeai	Oh you hurt me
Diu ngalla Diu	Here it is, here

Daringal	His
Da, mung	A Cap
Eeneera	To throw — or throw thou
Ecora	Men, or people
Eaneea	There
Ghar,awang	A Paddle
Ghoolara — Ghoolara mung	Cross or Ill-natured, Very Ill-natured
Garree	To Cough
Gittee Gittee	The Armpit
Gnarra	A knot or to tie a knot
Gnamul	A stone sinker to a line
Godgang	A Pidgeon
Gniana	To breathe
Gou Gou	More More
Guauyo	Bye and bye or Stop
Gwee ung	Fire
Karadigan	Doctor (they call all our surgeons by this name)
Kai	What do you say
Karal	A snood to a fishhook
Kubbera	The Head
Karungan	The Nail of the finger
Kadiaba	Lame, or the limps
Karooma	A Fish called by us the Black Bream
Kaadien	The spell on the Womara or throwing Stick
Kaadienmadiou	I kaadianed it (that is, I put that spell on the womara)
Kuama	To Dig
Murry	Large
Mulnaoul	Tomorrow
Mulla	A man or husband
Mu or Mu diu	What? or What's this?
Maana	Take it up
Muama or Maanoro	I don't understand you
Mu kiara	What's the name
Miteeanga or Miteea	Stop a little stop
Mu Murry	Now Many
Maan	To take
Maanma Wooroo	Go fetch it
Ngang deea or Nang deeakiara	What's the Name of this person or thing?
Ngairee	To bring
Naa	To Sea
Naabuou	I will see
Nangura bu Diami	She is asleep
Ngullia	A friend or Ally in Battle

162

Ngan ngieni kiara	What is your name
Nago	The Nose
Parribugo	Tomorrow
Parrabuggy	I have lost it
Pyomu	Sing
Pyuatiatu	Talk
Pana	Rain
Peyi	To speak
Pierbani	Burnt
Paratbunga	Open the door
Pograbanie ⎫	Broken to pieces, as a ship or boat
Pagrabaala ⎭	On the Rocks
Tabonga	To Yawn
Tieeringang	To Sneeze
Taa boarool boorool	To Gape
Taamooly	To change names (which they are very fond of doing)
Taaiabalang	Good (as to Eating)
Tamara	To wipe the hands
Tanie	To tie — or tie thou
Tamura	The Hand
Tarraburra	Day
Werowee	A Child
Wogul	He (Third person sing.)
Wauliweea	To Return
Worrong-wooree	On this side (the water)
Weeanadooroo	Bye and Bye
Wuling	The lip
Waulo	The chin
Womara	To Run, as an animal, To fly, as a spear (It particularly means the throwing stick)
Waura	Rascal (or the like)
Wauranga	When
Waunia	A Lie or falsehood
Waunadiemi	You did lie
Waaragal	The Mackerel
Weary	Bad
Yagoona	Today or now
Yen	To go — or walk
Yenmaarie	May I go
Yenmaou	I will go
Yarrsboonie	Mind your Work
Yerung	A Tree
Yuraboabo	Bye and Bye

9. Two letters from David Blackburn to P. G. King, 13th October and 25th October, 1788 (P. G. King Letter Book, Norfolk Island, 1788-1799, M.L. C/187)

Sir,

After a passage of 12 days I am arrived with The Golden Grove with 21 Men and 11 Women Convicts, a Mr Dunavan (midshipman of the Sirius), a Sergeant and Corporal of Marines and 5 Privates and 2 Gardeners. I have brought with in the Supply's Jolly Boat and a Boat Crew, the Ship's Long Boat and a 5 oared Cutter.

Previous to my sailing the Governor mentioned my keeping some of the Convicts on board to assist in getting out provisions etc., and if you approve of it, I wish to keep four of them for that purpose, namely Joseph Robinson, Thomas Watson, Edward Smith and William Dring. They are young single Men and have been used to the Sea. The Convicts are all victualled up to Friday next *included* viz. and next Saturday is Sailing Day. I hope you will receive all the Live Stock safe on Shore. They are all in a thriving condition. I am sorry to inform you that one of the Goats died on Wednesday last, in kidding.

Should the weather prove very fair I apprehend the Long Boat will be very useful. I have drawn up the enclosed signals for your alteration or approbation and I am, Sir,

With Great Respect,
Your humble Servant,
D. Blackburn.

Golden Grove
13th October, 1788.

Dear Sir,

I send you the sketch of the island to which you are heartily welcome if you think it worth your acceptance. The compass is drawn without allowing the variation. That is about 12 east. The soundings are in fathoms.

N.N.W. about 5 miles from Duncombe Bay there is a Bank of coarse Sand and Coral with 16 and 17 fathoms on it between which, and the Anchorage places there is 25 fathoms. There are also soundings S.E. from Phillip Islands coarse and rocky, from 35 to 25 fathoms at least, 4 leagues off at which distance it is fouled and shoaled so that *that part wants examining.* I should not be surprised if there is any shoal water there and I rather think there is. The bearings when at anchor in Diamond Bay were Cook's Rocks, and the Rocks off Port Howe, East by South and off North. The landing place south distance off shore, a mile. The depth 19 fathoms coarse Sand and Coral. The best Anchorage in Cascade bay is with the great Cascade S.W. and the N.E. point of the island S.E. distance off shore about 1½ miles 18 and 19 fathoms, tolerably good ground. If you anchor near or in, you will have less water and very foul Ground. Cascade bay is a very good road in the strong S.W. winds and very smooth. The Landing is easy, as is the access to the Island.

As the Ebb goes 9 hours to the eastward, very strong and coarse, therfore anchoring in Sydney Bay, on account of the boats etc. with the body of Nepean Isle east south-east half-east, or east by north.

North north-east half-east
south-west by west and the west end of Phillip Isle south-east *19 fathoms but here the ground is rocky.* The best anchorage is with the middle of Nepean Isles east north-east half-east. The west end of Phillip's Island south by east the outermost breakers off Point Ross north-west by west half-west — the flagstaff north N.E. half E and Collins Hood, N.E. by E. 17 fathoms clean ground and an excellent large cliff to the eastward of Point Ross which cliff, I think should be distinguished by some name.

The tides round that island are very strong, and from the observations I have been able to formulate and the difficulty we always found in the Supply in getting from Cascade Bay, round to Sydney Bay, whichever end of the island we tried at, has given us every reason to believe that the flood sets south south-west and the ebb north north-east. It flows 7 o'clock, or thereabouts, in Sydney, and Cascade Bays. Now, as the ebb runs 9 hours north north-east it strikes directly against that point of the island off which the large breaker lays, and this point splits the tide. It rushes to the eastward towards the former course of S.S.E. and the other part S.S.W. past Alison Bay round the West end of the island and thence N.N.E. so that in coming from the North side of the island (in case the wind gives a slant) you have the tide right ahead whichever end of the island you attempt to get round. As to the Flood it runs but three hours and with but little strength.

Yours sincerely,
D. Blackburn.

I have but little of Ball Bay but am determined to overhaul it before we sail if the weather admit, etc.

Golden Grove
Sidney Road
October 25th 1788.

10. A surviving letter written after his return to England. 1793

London 17th September, 1793

My Dear friend,

By this you will be informed of my appointment to H.M. Ship Dictator—Captain Dodd. I received my warrant this morning and must join her at Chatham immediately—she is fitting out for the coast—I therefore wish to have my things as soon as possible and as water carriage at present is dangerous I should wish them to be sent by the London Waggon directed to me at the Black Bull Inn, Bishopsgate, London from whence they will be safely sent to me at Chatham.

I shall want everything you have so long had the trouble of (except the large chest, the telescope, and the mess utensils, etc.) for which I shall have no use at present and they will serve me again whenever I am appointed to a Division again—I know not how you will manage the package of my box of books and charts, etc., with the cott, bed, bags of great coats, etc.,—but I must leave it to you, who I know will do everything this proper—and whatever expenses you may be at for packages, coverings, cartage, etc., I beg you will let me know. I hope you and Mrs H. are in good health and sincerely wish the old ship may turn out much to your advantage. You will remember me to my acquaintances at Plymouth and believe me to be with great esteem yours sincerely,

D. Blackburn.

I shall be glad to hear from you as soon as possible. You will direct to me etc. etc., at the Mitre, Chatham.
Let me know what you know of D.

Mr Richard Harper,
No. 40 Clowance St.,
Plymouth Dock.

APPENDIX II

Note on Lieutenant Henry Lidgbird Ball, R.N., Commander of the Supply.

Although Lieutenant H. L. Ball played a very important part in the foundation of Australia, nothing is known of him prior to his appointment as Commander of the Supply, except that he had previously sailed with Blackburn in the *Victory*.

During the period of the first settlement, there is considerable mention of him in the official records. He frequently sat as a member of the Criminal Court and he took part in various expeditions on the mainland. On one occasion, he and Lieutenant Johnstone captured an aborigine alive, and he was among a small party that surveyed Broken Hill in 1789.

On the 5th April, 1790 it was Ball who brought back to Sydney Cove the tragic news of the loss of the *Sirius*, and it was he who commanded the emergency voyage to Batavia on the 17th April for more supplies. Later that year, he became ill, and Blackburn assumed his command. In fact, Ball's life was despaired of in December, 1790. Though he survived, he asked to be allowed to return to England the following spring. Eventually, he sailed for home in the *Supply* on the 26th November, 1791.

APPENDIX III

Note On The Aborigines

The aborigines, the original human inhabitants of Australia, probably came from South-East Asia about 12,000 years ago. It is thought that they brought with them the dingo — a wolf-like Australian dog. They possess physical features which clearly differentiate them from all other races of mankind and their blood-group pattern is unique among the peoples of the world. This suggests that they originated from a small isolated group of people. In Australia, they formed tribes and were driven by drought to be nomadic in nature.

At the time of the first white settlement, there were probably about 500 languages being used by them — but these may very well have stemmed from one original language. They also used a most effective sign-language which came into being owing to the necessity of keeping quiet when stalking their prey.

It is now recognised that the Aborigines have a genuine artistic expression of their own. Governor Phillip first reported their rock-engravings which were found near Port Jackson in May 1788. Similar engravings have been found in abundance in various parts of the Continent and Aboriginal art has now gained a world-wide recognition.

The population in the year 1788 was thought to have been about 300,000. At the last published census (1954) there were 26,363 full-blooded aborigines left.

BIBLIOGRAPHY

Reference has been made to the following works and where actual quotations have been used, due acknowledgement has been paid in the text.

History of Norwich	P. Browne
The Story of Australia	Professor A. G. L. Shaw
Australia	Professor Spate
The Foundation of Australia	Dr Eris O'Brien
The New World of the South	W. H. Fitchett
The Story of Sierra Leone	F. A. J. Utting
Early Explorers in Australia	Lee
Australia	Griffith Taylor
Australia—Her Story	Kylie Tennant
Sydney Cove	Dr John Cobley
Sydney	Brian Kennedy
The Diaries of a Country Parson	Ed. John Beresford, 1924
Margaret Catchpole	from the introduction by Clement Shorter

Index